forward those of us with white privilege must be made uncomfortable in order to see what has been unseen for too long. This
book should be required reading for all those in a position of
seniority in our society, as well as those entering professions such
as medicine, to provide encouragement to anyone experiencing
what Dr Liang has and to help them feel less alone in
their struggles."

PROFESSOR THALIA ELEY
PROFESSOR OF DEVELOPMENTAL BEHAVIOURAL
GENETICS AT THE INSTITUTE OF PSYCHIATRY,
PSYCHOLOGY AND NEUROSCIENCE

"Having been good friends with Holan since our formative
days in medical school, it comes as no surprise that she would
write a compassionate book on mental health highlighting
issues of social, racial and gender inequalities."

PROFESSOR RAVINDRA GUPTA
PROFESSOR OF CLINICAL MICROBIOLOGY, CAMBRIDGE
INSTITUTE FOR THERAPEUTIC IMMUNOLOGY &
INFECTIOUS DISEASES

"With wry humour Dr Liang pinpoints the need that everyone
has to belong. She draws on observations over the years – the
struggles of those who come to her for help, the difficulty of
aiding those with mental health problems in the context of
the decline and atomisation of public services since 2010, and
personal reflections on her own place in society and on the
NHS. An exceptionally thoughtful blend that comes
together for great effect."

DAN ROSENBERG
EDUCATION & PUBLIC LAW SOLICITOR, LEGAL AID
LAWYER OF THE YEAR 2018

A SENSE

of

BELONGING

*How to find your place
in a fractured world*

DR HOLAN LIANG

𝕭

DISCLAIMER

The stories in this book are inspired by real events and real people, although details have been altered to protect their privacy.

Published in 2022 in the UK by Short Books
an imprint of Octopus Publishing Group Ltd
Carmelite House, 50 Victoria Embankment
London, EC4Y 0DZ
www.octopusbooks.co.uk
www.shortbooks.co.uk

An Hachette UK Company
www.hachette.co.uk

10 9 8 7 6 5 4 3 2 1

A CIP catalogue record for this book
is available from the British Library.

ISBN: 978-1-78072-468-3

Jacket design by Jon Gray

Printed and bound in Great Britain by Clays Ltd, Elcograf S.p.A.

This FSC® label means that materials used for the
product have been responsibly sourced

For my sisters, the best whole life companions
through time and continents

I can't stand you
I can't understand you
I won't understand you
I want to understand you
I understand you

Contents

Why we need to belong

'Mental health' is having a moment. In recent years, we have seen a transformation in the way people talk about the subject, with public figures like Prince Harry, Stephen Fry, Billie Eilish and even Boris Johnson breaking the taboos that have long surrounded it. During the Covid-19 pandemic, I think we must all have had our mental health challenged one way or another – whether through fears of contracting or spreading the virus, being separated from loved ones, facing job insecurities, the horrors of home-schooling, marital tensions brought on by intense proximity, or the tragic loss of a loved one. Mental health professionals are warning of the long-term legacy of the devastation wreaked by the coronavirus. But despite this wider recognition of its importance, what do people really know about 'mental health'?

I certainly knew little when I embarked on my journey to becoming a psychiatrist over two decades ago. For me then, the first picture of poor mental health that sprang to mind was a negative one – and I think this is still the case for many people today. Why would we think any differently, given the quintessential 'madman' image that literature, film and art have used for centuries to portray mental illness? Think of the bedraggled, toothless paupers of Bedlam; the crazy Victorian lunatic burning down attics; or the perverse violence of the intellectual psychopath pairing human organs with a chilled Chianti. Very often, even now, if the mentally unwell are not depicted as violent, rampant killers, they are cast as weak creatures to be pitied, infantilised and institutionalised. These images are society's collective worst fears about the human condition neatly projected onto the most vulnerable in society. Excluding people for whatever reason helps differentiate ourselves from 'them' – those that don't belong – so that we can be protected from the need to confront our own insecurities. When it comes to mental health, at the root of our fear is the knowledge that we share the same human condition, making us all capable of tipping into 'insanity'.

My own route into mental health and a career in psychiatry did not have the most auspicious beginnings. I had not set out to be a psychiatrist, or even a doctor, but somehow mental health found me, in more ways than one. The beginning of my journey took place in Taiwan, on a hot summer's day over 40 years ago.

The sticky heat of summer in Taichung is unbearable even when standing still, and far worse on a day when you are traipsing to the passport office and waiting in line for hours on end. That afternoon, my new plastic sandals were pinching my heels and my hair was plastered to my forehead with sweat. 'I want an ice lolly!' I whinged to my mother, pretending I could no longer walk. After a while of this, and as many huffs and uncomfortable nasal sounds as I could muster, my exasperated mother relented. 'Oh fine! We'll stop at the next shop.' This was a surprise to me, as my thrifty mother rarely let us have treats. But after a morning spent busting red tape, she probably felt we deserved one – a reward to celebrate her success at finally securing the right papers to enable us to join my father in Great Britain. What an adventure that would be! A new chapter in our lives. We turned the corner of the block and, to my glee, there was the gaudy flashing light of a shop that might sell ice lollies. Instantly, I regained full use of the muscles in my legs, broke free from my mother and ran at top speed towards the shop front.

As I reached the entrance, I saw him. Square on the pavement to the left of the shop sat a man in a cage. Instant fear stopped me in my tracks. I wanted to scream, but my dry mouth could not bring up a sound. I took a step back, and although it was only a minute before I felt my mother's hand on my shoulder, I still remember the moment that he looked at me, and I looked at him. Tears of distress were stinging my eyes and I felt a warm trickle make its way down my leg. Looking back on that encounter, I realise that my terror of the man was heightened by my sense of hatred and loathing for the weakness he had evoked in me.

In reality, he had done nothing but look at me in curiosity. But in my young mind, he had leapt out of the shadows and snarled at me. I imagined him rattling at the bars of the cage. His hair was matted, he was clearly unwashed; and he was certainly hunched and cowering. The whites of his eyes were not white, but yellow, matching the few remaining teeth in his mouth. In my runaway mind, he wore a loin cloth and chewed on a bone like a caveman. His pupils spun wildly, and he made guttural noises like an injured animal.

This was my first encounter with a person suffering from mental health problems.

Thankfully, our collective willingness to understand mental health is shifting. And with it, the old stigma and negative representations of mental illness are slowly but surely being chipped away. Contemporary films like *A Beautiful Mind*, *Black Swan* and *Still Alice* have offered sensitive, three-dimensional portrayals of lives unravelling that are quite different from the films of the past. Most people these days recognise that poor mental health is a problem that will likely touch each and every one of us at some point in our lives, personally or vicariously.

While knowing this to be true statistically as a psychiatrist, it was a different matter when I experienced mental health problems myself first-hand. For many doctors, and particularly psychiatrists, it is extremely difficult to acknowledge that our own mental health is as fragile as that of the people we treat. Certainly, few people, even close colleagues, have been aware that in my own dark times, I have been seconds away from being a suicide statistic. In the years since I was at my lowest ebb, I have had the chance to think about the hows and whys of my own experiences and the indelible effect that poor mental health has had on my life. What happened to the confident teenager, the diligent junior doctor and the doting mother? How could she have ended up on the precipice of a third-storey window ledge? But of course, she could. Because she is only human, looking to belong, like your neighbour, colleague, mother, father, sister and brother and – dare you think it? – like you.

It sometimes takes a shock to make you take stock of your life. Experiencing chest pain, for example, is the quickest way to make people re-evaluate their diet and exercise. For me, as a psychiatrist, acknowledging my own less than perfect mental well-being was difficult, and left me contemplating more deeply the causes of mental health problems in general and what can be done to help. As a psychiatrist, at dinner parties, the question I get asked most after 'Ooh, are you going to analyse what I say now?' is 'So what brings on mental health problems in the first place?' Of course, there is no easy way to respond to this, because just as with physical health problems like cancer and heart disease, the answer is multifactorial and can vary from one person to the next. What is clear is that both nature and nurture have a big part to play. My own background in behavioural genetic research makes me appreciate the importance of genetic vulnerability in the development of mental health problems. I've read, written or presented enough papers involving brain scans, genetic markers, inflammatory markers and double-blind drug trials to be convinced that biology is crucial. However, as a human as well as a clinician, what has interested me most in listening to my patients day after day, month after month and year after year are the common environmental themes that their stories reveal: the feeling of being 'an outsider', of not fitting in, be it in their families, their schools, their workplaces or society. Many tell me of their nagging and shameful thoughts, a surprising number of which can be traced back to a single soundbite, a comment uttered by an angry parent, a sibling's dig or a playground taunt – words which have now metamorphosised into internal voices that haunt them day and night: 'You're not good enough', 'You're a freak', 'You're fat and ugly', 'Go back to where you came from'; in essence 'You don't belong'.

Through their experiences, I have come to understand that genetic vulnerability aside, what often matters most in the preservation of mental well-being is our sense of who we are (our identity) and where we 'belong'. The word 'belong' means to feel happy or comfortable in a group or situation. This definition risks making it sound like a fairly casual, straightforward thing. But as all of us know, the feeling of belonging – whether it be in someone's heart, in a place or a community – has deep roots within us and reaches into every aspect of our lives. Almost universally, our first experience of belonging is within our family. As we mature, we tend to seek a wider feeling of connectedness, with friends, colleagues, partners and society at large. The feeling that we belong – to someone, somewhere – is so important to us as human beings that psychologist Abraham Maslow, in his well-known 'Hierarchy of Needs', rated it the third-most crucial human need (after physiological needs, for example food, water, warmth, and physical safety). It's a need that is found across all cultures. US psychology professors Roy Baumeister and Mark Leary recognised it as the driver for much of human behaviour, including love, friendship, power and achievement.[1] Fitting into a larger group allows us to feel part of something bigger and more important than ourselves. Belonging, then, is a sense that we have roots and a purpose, that we are a valued member of a family, group or society; that we make a contribution. In essence, belonging validates and confirms to us that we matter, which is why it is so central to human happiness.

Certainly, it has obvious evolutionary advantages. Way back, in the early years of human life, the need for protection and care from others in our tribe likely meant that natural selection favoured those with a strong inclination to connect; and over millennia this has resulted in humans being hardwired with an intense desire to belong. Added to this, for centuries societies have encouraged 'belonging' as a means for social cohesion and control. The result is that the vast majority of us are highly adapted to seek it. Think honestly about how much of your day-to-day behaviour is driven by a desire to be liked, gain approval or have your status affirmed by those around you, and you can easily fathom the importance of belonging. Conversely, its absence can lead to loneliness, rejection and alienation – feelings strongly linked to shame and humiliation, the most damaging of human emotions. Understand this, and it is easy to appreciate how, without belonging, people can suffer not just mental but also physical ill-health.

After training in adult psychiatry, I specialised in child

psychiatry and wrote a parenting book with a focus on encouraging parents to build resilience in their children by understanding who they are as individuals and championing them in whatever they chose to do.[2] In my decades of clinical practice, I have come to realise that this sense of being understood, supported unconditionally and accepted for who we are (warts and all), is a requirement not just for children, but for us all. It is something that we need throughout our lives.

A few years ago, during a challenging period of my own, I realised that I was carrying the same 'baggage' as my patients – the sense that we didn't belong. As a child immigrant to the UK, 'Go back to where you came from' was an inevitable playground taunt. The first time it happened, having been schooled in biology rather than racism, I thought that the 'friend' was suggesting that I crawl back through my mother's vagina – which seemed like an odd and intensely uncomfortable request. It was only when the true meaning was explained to me that the shame hit, and ever since, like so many British BME people, I have carried that shame within me, like a dirty little secret, an Achilles' heel in my resilient armour.

It's not just because I have a 'weird' name; I am also a slitty-eyed, bat-eating, cockle-picking immigrant. I make my kids practise piano six hours a day and they get a good spanking if they don't bring home A* grades. If I am out with my children, I get mistaken for the nanny; and for the cleaner if I answer the door at home. And you can imagine what I got mistaken for in my younger days when I went on holiday with my white husband in Thailand. I have always been considered hard-working, but not, since childhood, 'talented'. I am at times 'too submissive' and at others 'too pushy', but never 'just right'. And perhaps that's why I understand my patients with mental health problems: I share their longing to belong.

In this book, I explore the reasons, ranging from the

socio-political to the deeply personal, why many of us may feel that we don't belong, and I look at how, by recognising and understanding the roots of the problem, we can come to a sense of self-acceptance and hopefully, connection. In the first few chapters, I discuss the different ways in which our connections with others can be impaired. What are the mental health consequences if our families are not able to offer us a sense of belonging or teach us the importance of connection? What if the people around us do not share our values? Do we swim against the tide, and if so, at what cost? What happens if we pretend to be people that we are not? And finally, what happens when we lose our friends, families or occupations, and how does that challenge our sense of belonging?

In the second part of the book, I examine the reasons why some people are more vulnerable to suffering a lack of connection than others, whether it's because their brains are wired differently from those of the majority, or because their lives have been marred by unfortunate and traumatic circumstances which shatter their sense of belonging, or by alienation, which both causes and perpetuates their mental ill health. These situations are far more common than you might think. I share stories inspired by real people and demonstrate how and why a lack of belonging contributed to their mental health problems.

Finally, I think about what we can do to help – both as individuals and as society at large. Recent world events, divisive rhetoric and anti-immigrant propaganda have challenged all our notions of belonging. The coronavirus pandemic has had profound effects on global mental health, as strategies to combat its spread have forced people to be physically disconnected from their loved ones, leading to an epidemic of isolation and loneliness. Going beyond this, the emotions unleashed by the death of George Floyd, and by the rise in

Islamophobia and hate crimes against East Asians have high-lighted the longstanding alienation felt by many members of our society. The murder of Sarah Everard has led to women, who form the majority of the population, wondering if they matter at all. Mental health professionals are braced for an upsurge in demand for their services. Yet, from my experience of working in mental health, I can tell you that it will never be enough to rely on our services to put people back together: we need a society that works to help people find themselves and their place to belong. We need to prevent the cracks appearing in mental wellness from the start, rather than simply cement over them as they appear. Perhaps, as in the case of the man in the cage back in Taichung, we need to get mental health and exclusion in all its forms out in the open and hold society to account.

In recent years, much of the discourse about mental health has placed an emphasis on encouraging people to talk about their problems: this is great, but wouldn't it be even better if we could prevent the problems occuring in the first place? Wouldn't people made redundant or humiliated at work prefer a job in which they are valued and respected rather than an opportunity to talk to someone about how they feel? Wouldn't a lonely child prefer a friend or an engaged parent to a coun-sellor? What are the steps that we need to take to reach that kind of society?

In my view, I think we need to rally around the words of Jo Cox: 'We are far more united and have far more in common with each other than things that divide us.' There are actions every community can take to work towards creating a sense of universal belonging: in homes, schools, and in the workplace.

As for what we can do to help ourselves as individuals, throughout this book I also look at the myriad ways in which we can improve our own sense of belonging. Like physical health, good mental health takes time and effort to maintain; sometimes it can be badly damaged, but our minds also have a remarkable ability to heal and recover, and just as healthy diet and exercise can improve physical health, there are things that we can all be doing to restore and maintain our mental well-being. I'm not just talking about yoga and meditation, which may be good means of disconnecting from stress; but rather ways of reconnecting meaningfully with those around us and, most crucially, with ourselves. Because, through my own experience, I have discovered that belonging is inextricably linked to identity and how we understand ourselves. Our sense of identity is often influenced by how others view us, and in seeking to belong, we may warp some aspects of our individuality to try and please people and fit in with them. One day, we might even realise that we no longer recognise, or even like, who we have become; that we are lost. Recovering from this requires hard introspection and work, involving re-prioritising what is important to us as individuals. I hope that by sharing my personal journey of becoming content with my authentic self, I can help you as you embark on yours; because the most important discovery I have made is that 'where we belong' is not dependent on whether others accept us, but ultimately on whether we accept ourselves.

Throughout, I aim to demonstrate that mental well-being is not to be taken for granted and that it affects people of all colours and from all walks of life, and at any age. My journey to understanding started when I took the first small step, perhaps the hardest of all, by facing my fear rather than recoiling to safety. I was lucky that, from the start, I had a good role model in my mother.

Although Taiwan is now a developed country, 40 years ago it was an Asian tiger economy yet to offer affordable healthcare for all, and certainly with no tangible mental healthcare policy. The boy in the cage – for behind the dirt he must have only been in his teens – was the son of the shopkeeper who duly handed over the lollies that my mother bought and used to console me. My mother found out from the boy's father that he had been born 'slow' and had become erratic and unpredictable in his behaviour. He required supervision at all times lest he should run into traffic or lash out at someone in his path who didn't understand him. Today, he would have a diagnosis of severe intellectual disability and autism. The family could not provide the supervision needed as they had to work in the shop to keep a roof over their heads, so had come up with the idea of the cage in order to keep an eye on him and ensure that he was safe. Their son liked to watch the passing traffic; it seemed to calm him, which is why they put him out at the front of the shop rather than in the back. They were sorry if he scared the little lady. We left the shop, and as we did so, my mother reached into the cage and handed the boy a lolly. In that moment, he smiled. And my fear dissolved. Although it would be decades before I thought of mental illness again, a key had silently turned, and my mind opened: we are all human. We are all longing to belong.

PART ONE

Why we don't belong

1

Emptiness: absence of first connections and faltering family ties

The Hunger Games

To achieve the warm, healing feeling of belonging, we need to more than merely interact with other people. We need to give and receive understanding, acceptance and attention. However, our capacity for doing this is dependent on our having been loved and supported in our childhood. To understand the critical importance of early love and support, please consider *The Hunger Games*.[*]

Imagine being Katniss Everdeen standing on the podium at her first Hunger Game. You would feel anxiety and fear for sure, but there would also be a part of you that knew that you'd been trained in preparation for this moment. Haymitch Abernathy, the District 12 tribute mentor, has taught you how to find water, how to scavenge for food, how to make alliances, how to attract sponsors, how to fight – essentially how

---

[*] This is a fictional reality game show where people (called tributes) from different districts fight to survive in a jungle enclosure, with the victor being the last person alive.

to survive. You would be aware that Haymitch was watching your every move on screen and would provide help if he could. In short, although you were about to face the biggest ordeal of your life, you would have the sense that you were not wholly alone, that someone was on your side, looking over you and championing your success at every turn.

I don't wish to equate real life to a televised fight to the death for purposes of light entertainment, but it is a useful analogy to bring home the critical importance of parenting, whether that be from a biological parent or parental figure, to our mental survival. The marvellous Katniss Everdeen was unquestionably talented, but without Haymitch and the District 12 team firmly in her corner, she would likely have died early on. Katniss trusts Haymitch and, even in her darkest hours, she knows that he is looking out for her. By sending her medicine, he mends her not only physically but emotionally. Like many parents, myself included, Haymitch is a flawed human being, but his support of Katniss is without a doubt the basis of her success in surviving the Hunger Games.

Now imagine if Katniss had been made to enter the Hunger Games arena without the District 12 team behind her. In fact, imagine yourself in that situation. It would be difficult not to feel frightened and alone. Knowing that other people in the arena were out to kill you would lead you to feel mistrustful and aggressive, especially if you had not been advised that making alliances is helpful, or taught how to go about doing so.

You'd be acutely aware that your survival was dependent on yourself alone; that there was no help or safety net. You might feel that events were out of your control; the fear would be immense and overwhelming. You'd feel confused about the strategies of the game and would need to develop your own plan, but without someone to reassure and guide you,

you'd second-guess or doubt yourself over and over. To make things worse, you'd observe that other contestants had a team supporting them, providing advice and resources, which would make you jealous, resentful, bitter and angry. You might feel inferior to the other tributes and wonder why you did not have the same support as others – was it because you were worthless and undeserving? You might have a perpetual feeling that you are doomed.

These are the same emotions that many children feel when they have no one loving, guiding and supporting them. They muddle along as best they can, but over time (particularly if no adult mentor in the form of a relative, teacher or youth worker steps into this role), they become adults who believe that they are 'unlovable', 'not good enough' and 'undeserving of love'. This is an awful empty feeling and can go some way to explaining why some people never achieve the satisfaction and contentment of belonging in their lifetime. Despite immeasurable talents, many fail under these circumstances.

First connections

For most of us, our first experience, and therefore our first understanding, of what it means to belong will be shaped by the relationships within our families. This group of people is unique to us in that we have no choice about entering it. Biology offers us a helping hand in our first quest to belong, often by virtue of giving us similar physical, physiological and psychological traits to our parents and siblings, and society ensures that our membership card to this exclusive club has a long expiry date – 18 years or more. Most of us are locked in for life. However, this can make it all the more painful if our family, the people that are closest to us, do not understand

and are not, or cannot be, supportive of us.

The requirement for at least one relationship involving unconditional love and acceptance, especially as an infant, is the basis of 'attachment theory', first described by the psychiatrist John Bowlby in the 1950s. Having this bond is viewed as a necessary foundation for us to be able to grow into a secure adult capable of mutually caring relationships, a requisite for belonging. Unlike Bowlby, who was adamant that this attachment relationship could only be provided by mothers, most modern-day psychiatrists recognise that it need not be maternal; indeed, it need not be parental. Children may be raised by grandparents, aunts, uncles, foster or adoptive parents, who are just as able to offer the necessary closeness and connection for attachment – it is not the biology that is important, but the unconditional love of someone who is always there when needed. But for ease, forgive me for referring to this person/relationship as a parental one henceforth, as such a provider of love to children is de facto a 'parent figure'.

It is sometimes easy for people to see the parenting role as one of a physical 'provider' (providing home, food, toys, books, clothes, music lessons, schooling), but a parent is more than just a credit card. There are situations – in the case of children living in extreme poverty, for example – where food and safety concerns may be the priority, but the primary role of parents is to provide emotional warmth and support, to be a moral compass and give guidance; often what we would bundle up with the word 'love'. Children without a secure, unconditionally loving parental figure will frequently show emotional and behavioural problems as a precursor to mental illness – children like Hayley, for example.

Seven-year-old Hayley was brought to clinic by her legal guardian Lisa. On that first visit, Lisa described one recent incident when she had been cradling a friend's baby, being supportive of her, and saying, 'She's so beautiful', as any friend would, and Hayley had asked, 'Do you love her more than you love me?' To which Lisa responded casually, 'Of course not, Hayley, don't be daft.'

For Hayley, though, Lisa's act of affection for another child was a gross betrayal. An uncontrollable anger was growing inside Hayley, from where she didn't really know. She only knew that her whole being ached with rage. She didn't know that this feeling was called 'jealousy' and stemmed from a fear that Lisa would leave her. She couldn't articulate how important it was to keep Lisa bound to her, because of the pain of being alone she had experienced in the past, and she didn't know how to control or direct her anger except in harmful ways. She wanted to lash out at Lisa – 'I am not daft. You are my mummy, not her mummy!' – but she couldn't because as much as she hated Lisa in that moment, she needed Lisa to love her. The baby had been the cause of this threat of being pushed away, and to stop that, the baby had to pay. When the women were not looking, she glanced over at the sleeping baby on the blanket and she pinched her hard on the leg. The baby cried. 'Snitch,' Hayley thought, and she ran away.

Hayley had been born premature to Natasha, who had been a victim of domestic violence and had used alcohol and illicit drugs throughout her pregnancy. It was known at birth that Natasha would not be able to look after Hayley, and her extended family had tried their best to prevent the baby from going into care. For the first year of Hayley's life, she was passed between various family members. Eventually, however, social workers approved Natasha's cousin and his wife, Lisa, as her legal guardians. A year later, when Lisa left her husband, Hayley went with her as Lisa was the only mother she had ever known.

Lisa described how Hayley would go up to children she

didn't know and want to take over their games. She would smack other children for no discernible reason. Lisa reported that, at two years old, Hayley had been clingy and when she was not given her own way, she would smack or pinch herself, or hit her head on the floor, but nowadays the aggression was targeted at Lisa. Hayley would call Lisa names, scream, slap and swear at her. Lisa was beginning to struggle, particularly as she now had her own four-year-old daughter, Maria. Hayley could be cruel to Maria and on one occasion had locked her in a room. Hayley's outbursts were often unpredictable, and Lisa felt that she had to 'walk on eggshells' at home in order to prevent triggering a tantrum that could last up to two hours.

In the last six months, Lisa explained, Natasha had returned on the scene, having been rehabilitated from drug and alcohol addiction. At their first reunion, Hayley had seemed happy to walk off with Natasha right there and then, as if Lisa's hard work parenting over the years had counted for nothing. Hayley now called Natasha 'Mummy' too, which riled Lisa. However, Lisa had agreed with the social workers that it would have been wrong to deny Hayley a relationship with her birth mother. So now, despite Lisa remaining her legal guardian, Hayley made weekly visits to Natasha's home, where she had a half-sibling, two-year-old James.

Lisa mentioned Hayley's distress at her situation, reporting that she'd said, 'Why me? I don't want to have two mummies.' More recently, she had told her teachers that she wanted to die, which had resulted in her referral to child mental health. It was clear to me that Hayley felt unconsciously torn as, although she was eager to know her birth mother, she felt loyalty to Lisa. Struggling to understand and articulate her divided loyalties, she could only comment that her family arrangement was unusual and how it made her feel.

Knowing Hayley's history can put her behaviour and

words into perspective. During her first year, she lacked a single stable, loving, long-term presence in her life. Although this changed when she went to live with Lisa, she soon experienced further instability when Lisa's marriage broke down and she lost her father figure. The birth of Lisa's daughter Maria brought further family changes, which Hayley struggled to manage. These fluctuations in family circumstances and the feeling of being usurped by siblings in the affections of parents are difficult to cope with for any child, but for children with a history of attachment problems, they can be all the more overwhelming.

Although Lisa was a kind and supportive guardian to Hayley, when she had initially agreed to take on Hayley's care, this had been envisaged as a partnership with her husband. Now the task fell to her alone. Of course, she swore blind to herself and others that she did love Hayley, and she certainly felt a sense of duty, aware that Hayley needed her after all that she had been through. And yet there were signs of her inability to commit to the little girl. Something had been stopping her from pursuing adoption, especially after she had her own daughter. What was it? She couldn't quite go there. There was no denying that Hayley was hard work, and when Natasha had come back into their lives, with her own little boy, there was a part of Lisa that wanted to ask, 'Why won't you take Hayley back now that you've got your act together?' and 'How come I'm looking after your child?'. Still, she pushed that thought to the back of her mind, feeling guilty for even considering it.

Hayley could see a tension between Lisa and Natasha and sensed that her future stability was somehow on more rocky ground than ever before. She wondered why James had been able to stay with Natasha, while she had been rejected. She thought this must have been because she 'was a handful'. Lisa sometimes said this on the phone to her friends when she thought that Hayley wasn't listening. It made Hayley feel sad, but deep down she knew it to be true. She sensed that both Lisa and Natasha had their own children who seemed to 'belong' to them more than she ever did to anyone. In the pit of her stomach, she had a gnawing feeling that she had no control over her future, that these women in their hushed phone calls with the social worker would be deciding her destiny and she would be passed along again; pieces of her heart being torn off at every exchange, a pass-the-parcel unravelling until there was only emptiness left.

The origins of insecurity

We gave Hayley a diagnosis of attachment disorder, as she didn't feel supported by an early love that was secure and irrefutable. Much is now understood about the way that a failure to make secure attachments as a child can progress into mental health difficulties in adulthood. Some children who have attachment disorder will have been subject to serious abuse and neglect (thankfully this was not the case for Hayley); but many more children suffer milder, subclinical difficulties from 'insecure attachment'.[3] These are children who do have a parental relationship but for whom, for a myriad of different reasons, this

---

* Insecure attachment style is reportedly present in 40% of the population, which is why it is important. The majority will not have any difficulties, but it may increase vulnerability to adapting to life stress. Subclinical insecurity and clinical attachment disorder are not discrete conditions but lie on a continuum with insecurity at the mild end, and attachment disorder at the severe end. Many of the emotions and behaviours overlap, but in clinical disorder the symptoms emerge at a younger age, are more extreme (e.g. involve higher levels of aggression) and are more entrenched (less likely to remit over time even with love and care).

relationship lacks warmth, is only lukewarm, or runs hot and cold. For these children, deficits in the parental relationship are not the direct cause of mental health problems (and problems are not an inevitability)* but their presence renders children more vulnerable to mental health problems given other genetic factors and/or life stressors.** What is concerning, however, is that these weaknesses in parental relationships often pass under the radar of professionals when a child's basic physical and safety needs are adequately met.

This vulnerability is often coded in innate insecurity, what psychoanalysts sometimes describe as a 'lack of sense of self', which can manifest as 'low self-esteem'. It's very rare for young children to go about declaring that they have low self-esteem, however, so child psychiatrists have to become detectives to identify proxies for it in infant and young-child behaviour. These clues might be found in excessive crying, for example, or aggression in response to a minor frustration such as spilling a drink. Children with good self-esteem view a small mishap like this as 'a one-off accident' or 'bad luck', unrelated to their ability, core value or worth. In essence, they have complete certainty that they will continue to be loved even if they make mistakes. Children with low self-esteem, on the other hand, are more likely to view misfortune as

---

* Early insecure attachment difficulties are often completely overcome by later experiences of love and care, but this is far less common in children with an attachment disorder.

** This is often referred to as the diathesis–stress model or vulnerability–stress model. An example of this would be when someone with a perfectionist personality (vulnerability) is faced with exam failure (stress), which then leads them to develop depression. Neither perfectionistic personality nor exam failure alone would have been a problem, but it is the combination that is pathogenic. Children will be more or less resilient to mental health problems depending on their personality traits, genetic make-up and early life experiences.

personal punishment or as an indicator of their inability to 'be good', something on which parental love is dependent. Some of these children might try to defend themselves from these types of hurtful thoughts by blaming others excessively instead. Bearing these insecurities in mind, it becomes easier to understand why these children can express their frustration through hopeless self-pity, aggression or both. The irony is that these responses tend to evoke irritation from adults ('Stop crying over nothing!', 'You're always blaming other people – go to your room!'), leading to rejection – an affirmation in the child's eyes of their core badness.

These types of mild behavioural problems were getting six-year-old Leah into trouble at home and at school. She was referred to clinic after her teachers, having noted that there were no known issues within Leah's family, queried whether she had a diagnosis of autism spectrum disorder (ASD). They reported aggressive behaviour with her classmates when she felt that she had been wronged, with a tendency to 'take things too far', and that other children had started to shy away from her. She would routinely refuse to do schoolwork, saying that it was 'too hard' when she had barely tried, and if she made a minor mistake in her work, she would cry, screwing it all up and saying it was 'rubbish'. For me, though, the most unusual thing about Leah was that she referred to her mother as 'Dr Forrester'.

Leah used this professional name for her mother so much that it initially caused me much confusion. Leah was brought to clinic by her father but spoke much of Dr Forrester's heavy involvement in her day-to-day life, from the food she ate to reprimands for her naughty behaviour. For a moment I thought that perhaps this family had won the health postcode lottery and the NHS care they were getting was particularly hands-on.

To clarify, I asked Leah who she lived with at home. 'I live with Daddy and Dr Forrester of course,' came the reply. It transpired that her mother, a radiologist, had suffered severe postnatal depression following the traumatic birth of Leah. Dr Forrester's depression was only picked up by midwives caring for her in her second pregnancy with Leah's younger brother Michael. Although she was then given treatment for her depression and her mood lifted slightly, she had never fully recovered and was still taking anti-depressant medication long-term, with her mood continuing to be affected by chronic physical health problems and work-related stress.

When I met Dr Forrester, she admitted that she could not remember much of Leah's first year of life, and that she was largely going through the motions that she felt were required of her. Her children's health checks and vaccinations were all meticulously up to date; but 'cooing and clucking' at children had never been her forte. She had worried for her career and admitted that she'd rather be sitting in a dark room analysing brain images than at the beck and call of a colicky baby. Dr Forrester explained that she suffered from rheumatoid arthritis and couldn't stand Leah's incessant chatter (which set off migraines), or the way she would bounce about the room, often bounding onto her lap for a big hug (triggering her arthritic pain). Dr Forrester said she preferred the company of Leah's calm younger brother Michael who could sit beside her quietly. Dr Forrester enjoyed reading to Michael, but these sessions were often disrupted by Leah divebombing onto the bed. Dr Forrester questioned why Leah couldn't be more like Michael, who was 'just so much easier to love from day one'.

Leah was not found to be on the autistic spectrum. Her core social and communication skills were intact, the only caveat being that her social abilities were a little clumsy. Clearly

Leah had difficulty in managing her emotions, which I felt was likely due to low self-esteem. She observed her mother and brother's intimacy and wanted to be a part of this, yet her advances were rebuffed. This had led to rejection issues which were played out in the school playground with aggressive responses when she felt left out by friends. Her attempts to win her mother's love by being loud and exuberant were successful at least in gaining negative attention, which on balance for Leah was better than no attention at all.

Parental depression is one of the most damaging of mental health conditions because it can prevent parents from providing warmth at the very time that humans need it most: in infancy and early childhood. There is evidence to suggest that maternal postnatal depression is a risk factor for children's mental health problems long into adolescence, increasing incidence of anxiety, depression, conduct disorder, attention-deficit hyperactivity disorder (ADHD) and learning difficulties.[4] For this reason, it is vital that parental depression is identified and help given quickly. Ideally, where a second parent is available and well, they can step in to provide the essential nurturing environment to infants.

Children who lack early social and intimate affection may suffer not only from low self-esteem but also from stunted social and emotional understanding. When agencies discovered severely neglected infants in Romanian orphanages during the Ceausescu regime, they found that they were all extremely impaired in their social ability – to the extent that their communication skills and empathy were on a par with those of children with moderate-to-severe autism.[5] Early isolation and lack of social stimulus had damaged their brain development so acutely that physical changes could be detected on their brain scans. In fact, though, very few of the children turned out to be 'genetically' autistic and some of them recovered fully or partially once they were fostered in loving homes.

As children grow, parental mental health remains important, and we know that children living with a parent with poor mental health are among the most vulnerable to developing psychiatric problems of their own.[6] It is likely that as well as passing on genes for mental health conditions, these parents struggle to keep themselves emotionally available for their children. Thankfully, in Leah's family, problems were not beyond repair. They had sought help and it was at hand. There were glimmers of normality in Leah's relationship with her father and Dr Forrester's relationship with her son was strong and loving. With the input of family therapy, it was hoped that Dr Forrester could be supported to become 'Mummy' to Leah as well as Michael.

Family connections

If parental warmth and care remain lacking, however, children with mild behavioural problems can evolve into angry and destructive teenagers, who will often reject parental advice and sanctions and deliberately engage in activities that they know their parents would not condone. It is commonplace for teenagers to rebel against their parents to some extent, but for those who have never felt the full power of parental warmth or the security of a seat belt around them, the heady teenage years can quickly spin out of control. It is not unusual for sabotage to occur and for parents to bear the brunt of hurt and blame.

I can vividly remember being approached by the parents of a teenage boy who had been cautioned by the police for arson. They were concerned that their son had gone 'off the rails'. They worried that it was because he was mixing with the wrong crowd at school, or that he had 'a mental health condition like bipolar disorder'. When I interviewed their son alone, I did not see any evidence of a psychiatric disorder. He was intelligent, insightful and articulate, albeit full of anger: 'I hate my parents. They never cared about me. I was raised by my nanny who has now gone back to Spain. I set fire to our house because I hate them, and I want to hurt them financially because that's what they care about most.' I have never forgotten that boy and his words, which echoed in my mind when I had my own children. When people asked me why I wasn't ready to return to work full-time once my younger child started reception, they were puzzled by my seemingly nonsensical response: 'I don't want my house to be burnt down.'*

The young arsonist is an extreme example, of course. But is there really that much difference between a teenager who wants to hurt others and a teenager who hurts themself? For many adolescents, where the act of hurting others is too radical or unconscionable, self-harm becomes an alternative option, one conscious, or more often unconscious, aspect of which (whether from reckless drinking, drug-taking, risk-taking, starvation or cutting) is that it serves a dual purpose: to hurt themselves and their families, the people they loathe the most.

The black sheep of the family

In all families – even loving ones – each member will have their own individual personality, which may bind or jar with

---

* This is not a statement against working parents at all; only that I recognised that my husband worked very long hours and if I also worked long hours in a demanding job, there would be little energy and mental capacity left between us to fully engage with our young children. My full thoughts on this topic are expressed in my parenting book.

others. I have always been very close to my mother – we just naturally get on, sharing the same outlook on life in general – whereas conversing with my father has always taken more work. It's not uncommon for dyads like this to form within families: mother and son in one camp vs father and daughter in the other, for example, as in Leah's family. And there is often flux in these groupings; for instance, my daughter and I pair up to ogle the actor Noah Centineo in the latest romcoms, while my son and I stay up late binge-watching *Stranger Things*, which his sister is too afraid to watch. This is normal and healthy. What can become troubling is when the family group always and consistently splits to exclude one member: the black sheep.

Although this can happen deliberately in instances of abuse (think of Cinderella), more commonly it is an unconscious process. Having family members who have similar personality types or share character traits is generally positive for cohesion; however, if one person is – or feels – left out, it can be immensely painful. The unathletic child in a sporty family, the tone-deaf child in a musical family, the albino child in a black family, a bookish child in a family that prefers watching TV (for example Roald Dahl's Matilda). These are clear divides, but feelings of exclusion in families can be caused by even the most subtle and unintentional of things. Just seeing oneself as different can feel like rejection if family members are not actively inclusive and don't work hard to keep all members feeling part of the team. It is the ongoing work of the family, or indeed any sort of group, to ensure that no one is left behind, and that all members are appreciated for the qualities they bring. Without this attentiveness, children may feel the need to edit or cancel any differing views and virtues they have in order to fit in; they may begin to suppress their differences, grow silent, try to take up less space and become less visible. This can certainly lead to stress, and sometimes even to self-sabotage at the conscious or unconscious level, which is what happened to my patient Ginny.

Ginny was a smart and articulate teenage girl from a family of high-achieving academics. Both parents had PhDs and dinner chat involved intellectual discussions about subjects such as the relative merits of Goethe, Bach or Wittgenstein. Ginny's sister Lindsay was applying to read natural sciences at Cambridge. Ginny had a preference for English over science, but had always been good at both. Her mother was eager to extol the many amazing achievements of both her children. She described Ginny frequently as 'gifted' (adding that Lindsay was 'not only gifted academically, but also socially and has a stunning boyfriend who plays county rugby'). However, while Ginny had 'excelled' at primary school and at the start of secondary school, more recently she had started to 'lose attention' in class. She would 'zone out' – particularly in maths; and more worryingly, she had started having what looked like seizures in the classroom, slumping sideways in her chair periodically, although she never lost consciousness. She was rushed to A&E, but an EEG showed no evidence of seizure activity. One morning, she suddenly found that she was unable to walk. She collapsed at each supported attempt to get her to stand. The family, in understandable panic, arranged for urgent neurological assessments. Meanwhile, the zoning-out episodes continued, sometimes two or three times a week, and Ginny worried about never being able to walk again and falling behind at school. Finally, after several more months of investigation and medical examinations, Ginny was told that there was no identifiable physical pathology, and she was referred to psychiatry to consider a psychological explanation.

Families often feel angry and let down when medical services cannot find answers to debilitating conditions. Like all of us, they want a problem diagnosed and medically treated so that they can get on with their lives. Unfortunately for psychiatrists, many of the people sent to see us via medical colleagues come in denial and disbelief that psychological problems are major contributors to their painful or incapacitating physical symptoms, and much of the work we do in clinic involves helping families to take a different, more holistic approach to resolving them.

The clinical term for physical symptoms – such as pain, lethargy, headaches, tummy aches, paralysis, seizures and even sometimes deafness and blindness – which are not caused by underlying physical disease is 'functional symptoms' (they are also known as somatic symptoms, conversion symptoms or medically unexplained symptoms). The underlying psychological pathology of functional symptoms is stress, anxiety and/or depression. For many people, it can be difficult to conceive that these conditions can result in physical illness and disability, but most of us have experienced how emotional pain can be felt physically. Anyone who has experienced a bereavement or the end of a relationship can understand that psychological pain can be as tormenting as physical pain and can actually cause symptoms such as headaches, tummy aches, lethargy and loss of appetite. Most of us also accept that stress can cause observable physical symptoms such as ulcers, acne and sleeplessness. Many of you will be familiar with two famous literary characters with functional symptoms: Clara from *Heidi* and Colin from *The Secret Garden*, both of whom experienced pain and paralysis following bereavement; and if you were one of many people who experienced an itchy throat or felt feverish at the height of Covid-19 pandemic anxiety, despite being Covid-negative, then you have experienced firsthand mild functional symptoms.

Sometimes it is obvious that our experienced symptoms

have a psychological basis. In the case of being royally dumped, for example, it is easy not to be too troubled by the physical symptoms of heartache, because we are aware of the psychological cause. We understand that to feel better we don't need MRI scans and medication; we need to get a haircut, practise self-love and invest in a killer revenge outfit. Functional symptoms become more of a problem when the cause is less obvious; when someone, for example, fails to identify or acknowledge that their overwhelming anxiety or depression is the cause of their lethargy and headaches. In this case, they may well feel that their physical symptoms have appeared 'as if from nowhere' when in fact, the seeds of emotional struggle have usually been there for some time.

Some people are more susceptible to converting psychological distress into physical symptoms. These include young children and people with a learning disability and/or ASD (where understanding of experiencing, expressing and managing emotions may be impaired), people from certain cultures (where mental health issues are highly stigmatised and may 'bring shame to the family') or, as in the case of Ginny, high-functioning people in very successful environments (where difficulty coping is perceived to be a sign of weakness).

Ginny was a smart cookie. Her memory was good, she was a good communicator and her family had always provided her with a rich milieu of books and conversation, so that she had the verbal ability to demonstrate intelligence to others. She had also been told from a young age that she was bright, and, feeling that she was not as conventionally beautiful as her sister Lindsay, this became the basis of her confidence and identity. She liked the certainty that there was an unspoken understanding that the Peters family were 'intelligent all-rounders', gifted academically, musically and athletically: she felt part and parcel of a strong family brand of success. She belonged. But secretly, unconsciously, she wondered if she was actually as smart as Lindsay. To be the less clever one would be a severe blow as she already recognised that she was not as pretty or popular as Lindsay. 'When will boys be calling on you, Ginny?' her mother would ask her playfully. It was not meant to be malicious or critical but Ginny found it so, particularly as she was beginning to wonder if she even wanted boys to call. She found herself looking at the girls in her class rather than at the 'dumb boys', but 'felt this to be wrong'. Since starting secondary school, she had noticed that she needed to spend more time on her studies to continue to be 'top of the class'. Sometimes she memorised answers and explanations rather than working things out; in this way she maintained her performance, but really, she wasn't quite keeping up. She had nightmares about being hunted down by wolves and constantly had a slight sense of foreboding – a feeling that she was hanging on by her fingernails.

For a while, she was able to dismiss these feelings as silly because her grades were still good, but over time, she lost her position at the top of the class. When her mother asked her about her latest score on her maths test, which was below her 'usual standard', instead of confessing that she was struggling to keep up in class, Ginny mentioned feeling her brain 'fog up'. Her mother took her to the GP, but her basic checks were all in order. Each time her mother and teacher told her that she was smart, the more Ginny believed the need to be smart was imperative, the less able she was to ask for academic help and the more she began to believe that perhaps she was physically ill.

Ginny's symptoms of non-epileptic seizures and paralysis were wholly unconscious. She felt genuine weakness and paralysis. These symptoms, though, were driven not by faulty nerves or muscles but by her anxiety about not living up to the expectations of success and normality that both she and her family harboured: high intelligence, top-level achievement, heterosexuality and mental resilience. Perhaps, after all, she didn't belong. If she was not intelligent, how could she be part of this family where intelligence counted for so much? This anxiety couldn't be openly acknowledged as, in her family environment of success, admitting anxiety over struggling academically was unheard of; and confusion regarding sexuality would require a difficult confrontation. The hard truths – that perhaps she was not as clever as everyone thought and that she might be homosexual – were too unbearable to contemplate. And so strong emotions were denied and suppressed, only to unconsciously resurface in the form of debilitating physical symptoms. The physical symptoms attracted sympathy and all sorts of positive attention and support. She was able to miss maths lessons if she needed to and of course illness and subsequent time off school conveniently provided a more palatable explanation for falling grades and 'failure'.

We were able to work with Ginny's family to help them understand functional symptoms and their psychological origins. When distress is accepted as a causative factor, it allows unconscious concerns to come to the surface and to be tackled one by one, and anxiety to be treated psychologically or pharmacologically. Happily, Ginny's fear of her family's response to her academic struggles and sexuality were unfounded; they were able to adjust their rhetoric, which had placed too much importance on academic and social achievement, and they were in fact overwhelmingly supportive on the issue of sexuality. Ginny's admission of anxiety was also positive as it turned out that her father had experienced severe anxiety symptoms when he was younger, but had shielded this history from her so as to present himself as a 'better role model' of success. Ginny's parents came to understand that the myth of the invincible parents was counter-productive, promoting in Ginny the false notion that struggling meant weakness and failure. With the admission of her father's anxiety symptoms, Ginny was able to feel that she was 'just like' her family members, after all: she belonged again. Over time and with physiotherapy, Ginny was supported to walk back into school.

It is much more productive for parents to be honest with their children about their true ability in any domain and to emphasise the value of working to their full potential (a value endorsed by psychologist Carole Dweck's theories on Growth Mindset,[7] of which more later), than to tie them to rigid markers of achievement. Ginny's anxiety was about academic prowess, but a child's fear of failure can apply to any area: sport, music, social ability. Being the 'least able' at something in a 'very able' family (or class) can be tough to take as comparisons are inevitable, however hard parents try to mitigate them. But it is always better to try and face these feelings and have open discussions about them rather than pretend that they do not exist or are somehow wrong. A spirit of openness, communication and support, regardless of each family member's ability, sexuality or personality, helps to ensure that children feel that they will always belong. The emphasis should be on making children feel loved for who they are, not for what they achieve, and regardless of their sexual preferences.

Strong foundations

I count myself extremely fortunate that my own parents and family provided me with the most secure start in life. Despite the financial hardships my parents faced, not for one moment in my childhood did I question whether or not I was loved by them. My father had been born in poverty in Taiwan. He frequently talked about being hungry on a daily basis in childhood. The majority of his ten siblings had started to work in factories straight after primary school; but he had been tagged as remarkably intelligent from a young age, and through hard work and stubborn perseverance (including walking barefoot for many miles to attend school), he managed to secure himself a university education and a job as an engineer. After that, he married my mother, a teacher from a middle-class family, and together they started their own family and saving for a better life. It took a decade for my father to save enough money to pursue his dream of a higher degree in Europe. In Taiwan in the 70s, an overseas degree was the highest mark of academic achievement and, for my father, whose background of abject poverty meant he had something to prove, this was perhaps his ticket to 'belonging'. He applied for a funded PhD at Swansea University in the UK.

If my parents' plan had ever been to return to Taiwan, it was bitterly thwarted by the fact that in the four years it took for my father to obtain his degree, all three of his children had become fully anglicised and been rendered illiterate in Chinese language and culture. With more knowledge of George Michael than Sun Yat Sen, we would all have found returning to Taiwan's highly competitive education system the equivalent of academic suicide. So, my parents did the next best thing: they moved onwards to London (where at least there was an established Chinese community) and my father acquired a short-term research contract at Imperial College. For a while we lived in university student accommodation and various rentals – my sisters and I three to a bed at times – before eventually throwing down roots in Cricklewood.

Although both my parents were well-educated, immigration

had meant a loss of earning potential due to their poor grasp of English. My early and middle childhood was lean on luxuries to say the least: dresses I'd outgrown were repurposed as smock tops to extend their use; the top halves of outgrown school uniform summer dresses were cut off and the bottom parts handsewn into skirts, which we wore with a jumper to hide the ruse. The few toys and books we owned were bought for pennies at the school fete. Each was treated with the utmost care and respect because we knew that if they broke or were damaged, there would be no replacement. But what we did not have in material wealth we gained in family unity, and within a few years of settling in London, my parents were able to begin a gradual ascent into prosperity as both could now connect to a burgeoning Taiwanese community that saw past their linguistic deficiencies and valued their skill sets.

By the age of 11, due to frequent house moves, I was on to my sixth school, so I was grateful when my parents finally took out a mortgage on a home, signalling the end of my nomadic childhood of making and remaking friends. After the move, my father started to work for a Taiwanese computer company, and my mother for a Taiwanese bank. Their English never improved significantly as it never needed to; they were immersed in a sub-community in which they belonged.

Inside-out parenting

As a child psychiatrist I cannot emphasise more strongly the importance of parental understanding, acceptance and support of children – it is like a mental health vaccine for the next generation. Of course, like any vaccine, it is not fully protective, but it certainly helps. Confident, happy children, armed with a dose of self-awareness, perseverance and humour, can overcome most challenges. It is my strong belief that our first experience of belonging, that of belonging in our own or adoptive family, is the most fundamentally important factor for mental health resilience. And that the primary goal of parenting should be to ensure that the children we raise are aware that they have a constant and unconditional support network for life. Without this consistency of emotional warmth and support, children can start to question if they are 'good enough'; and these seeds of doubt, if sown in childhood, can grow into long-lasting adult insecurities. Other parental factors that disrupt a child's security, such as an overly permissive attitude with no boundary setting or emotional guidance, can lead them to question if their parents care enough, which likewise challenges their belief about being loved. The irony is that these doubts about 'being good enough' or being loved are more likely to hamper 'success' or happiness outcomes than any innate weaknesses a child might have. We should be parenting children with their internal thought and emotional processes in mind: parenting from the inside out.*

Parent as you would have liked to be parented

Parenting is extremely difficult and demanding, but remember that what children need most, more than fancy clothes, toys and an expensive education, is *you*. Your love, attention, support and guidance. If you had a happy childhood in which you felt supported and loved, then just emulate what your parents did for you. If there were things you wish your parents had done differently, then enact these changes in your own

---

* For more on 'inside-out parenting', please see my parenting book of this name.

parenting. You are in the privileged position of knowing and understanding exactly how your children will feel if you do not.

Allow room for children to fail

In 2021, SpaceX's Starship crashed catastrophically – just like the eight prototypes before it. Few people were surprised, as Elon Musk has always pushed at the boundaries of what is scientifically possible, challenging mankind to do what has not been done before. But with each test flight, data is gathered, and improvements are made, and each subsequent failure is less spectacular and less likely to recur. Following this trajectory, I have no doubt that Elon Musk will eventually get tourists to Mars.

It is now widely accepted that most lasting success is based on persevering after failing at something, rather than never having failed at all. We should always allow room for our children to fail; indeed, as parents we should anticipate and prepare for this because, for all of us, no matter how smart, talented and popular we are, at some point failure is inevitable. We need to show our children that, far from being a negative, failure is a sign that they are operating at the upper boundaries of their ability, rather than coasting in an environment where they are certain of success.* Families and schools that challenge children at their individual levels, give them room to fail and then support them to learn from their mistakes and

---

* Of course, it is also unhealthy to allow children to flounder in environments that are too challenging – as a day-to-day experience of constant failure can cause lasting damage to self-esteem. This is why it is important to find the personal threshold of every child and help them achieve progress at a rate suited to them.

improve are more able to instil in children a feeling of self-belief, purpose and ultimately, belonging.

That said, while I believe that as parents, we have a responsibility to do our best, we all have our limitations due to our own life experiences and circumstances, and there is no benefit to self-flagellation if we get things wrong from time to time. This is inevitable, as parenting is the hardest job in the world, and ultimately, we are all only human. Therefore, we should allow ourselves the same room to fail as we afford our children, so that like them, we can learn from our mistakes. Promoting this message as widely as possible is crucial, as many parents are afraid to talk about their difficulties for fear of judgement by others. This of course reduces their ability to access help and support, and ultimately children suffer.

The media likes to portray parenthood to the masses as the ultimate joyful experience, when the reality is that most of the time, for most people, parenting can be a lot of stress, hard work and expense interspersed with brief moments of joy. All parents will struggle at some point (including me, and I am a child psychiatrist!). Parenthood is a life-long commitment and it can destroy marriages as well as bring people together. And in an overpopulated planet, where people have a free choice, there should certainly not be social pressure for people to start families. The wider this message is spread and the more normalised it becomes to talk openly about parental challenges, and how to get support and learn from others, the better parents we will all become.

2

Misfit: the anxiety of peer rejection and swimming against the tide

Beyond the family

It's the first day of Freshman year at Generic American High School. You've actually pulled off the outfit you've been putting together in your head for weeks, you weren't late for school despite having to cycle and you've made it to lunchtime. Well done, you. But now you have to face the moment that all teen/coming-of-age movies are built on: the cafeteria scene. Will you sit at 'the beautiful-but-bitchy cheerleader table', 'the laddish jocks table', 'the band-practice/mathletes/spelling-bee brainiac table' or 'the stoner/deadbeat rebel table'? Or worse, do you sit on your own? The reason this scene is so ubiquitous in movies is that the situation is universally recognised. Switch the scene to mid-90s university, swap the cheerleaders for trust fund blonds, the jocks for 'lads', the brainiacs for Doom players and throw in some goths and I've been there.

As children grow, that sense of family belonging that forms the bedrock of future relationships becomes insufficient to sustain a prolonged sense of well-being. There comes a point when they need to make their own way in the world and forge their own identities. They start to seek new connections and desire a wider sense of belonging, in a peer group. They're no longer looking for love, the marker of belonging in families, but validation, respect and esteem – markers of belonging in society at large.

While we can't choose our families, most of us can exercise an element of choice, even if limited, as to which peer group we join. Most of us don't think about how we ended up with the friends we have, as these decisions are often made instantly and subconsciously while holding a plastic lunch tray, but theoretically if we were to pick the process apart, it would have involved several steps:

1) Understanding our own identity.
2) Evaluating the identity of available groups to join.
3) Selecting a group that is a good match.
4) Mutual adjustment between ourselves and other group members.

Personally, I rather enjoy lunching alone; but none of us like feeling rejected, and for many people, the experience of having no one to sit with, of not being accepted by their chosen peer group, can quickly escalate into a feeling that they don't belong anywhere. Our identity, or who we are, is difficult to define as it encompasses how we view ourselves, how we are viewed by others and how we perceive we are viewed by others. Many of us are confused about our own identities as we all have multiple selves (for example, we may behave differently as a daughter, mother, wife, employee); we may see ourselves quite differently from how others see us and/or aspire to identities that are not based in our current reality.

Sometimes, even if our own identities are clear to us, the social environment available to us may not be a good match and we have to either 'make do' or suffer a lack of belonging. This is more likely to happen in homogenous and limited environments – in childhood, for example, where our school is often felt to be our 'entire world'; or in small towns and countries that lack diversity. In these sorts of environments, where the dominant group is likely to be somewhat inflexible, assimilation tends to be reliant on new members having to conform to existing group norms (think of university society initiation rites). What happens in these situations if we can't or don't want to conform and fit in with those around us? Feeling like a 'misfit' can be stressful and alienating, while active rejection by a group can mean we end up being lonely, bullied or even physically harmed. If belonging to a group is the ultimate 'feel-good feeling', then conversely, an inability to enter a group, or group rejection, can be the most painful of life's experiences.

Soft and hard peer rejection

According to her parents, Steph's problems had come on overnight following a mild flu, a month into starting at her new secondary school. One day, she was a calm, happy 11-year-old, and the next she had lost the ability to speak and would instead scream and cry when asked to get out of bed and ready for school. She would shake uncontrollably and cling to her bedpost till her knuckles turned white. This was described as a 'Jekyll and Hyde' transformation. Only after 10:30am, when the prospect of school was taken off the table, would Steph calm down and perhaps watch a movie or read a book. Even then, she continued not to speak, and the next morning the fearful trembling and anger would start again. The family had taken her to A&E, but the doctors had found no abnormalities in her EEG, brain scans or blood tests. They'd tried various antibiotics and anti-inflammatories, but these had not helped, and when she had been out of school for three months, they sought a psychiatric opinion.

Steph had done well at primary school and had a large circle of friends, with one particular best friend, Izzy. Their mothers had bonded in the playground on the first day of reception and the girls were inseparable from then on. Izzy and Steph had plenty of playdates and sleepovers, and the families even holidayed together. For Steph, it was hard when Izzy was sent to an independent secondary school, but the two friends would definitely keep in touch.

This account from Steph's parents did not indicate any social issues prior to her starting secondary school, and on the face of it, the onset of her difficulties did seem sudden. But when I scratched the surface, a different picture emerged. Izzy was a bubbly person, good-natured, smart and taught to be kind and diplomatic by her parents; the type who was 'head-girl' material. From reception, she had been encouraged and rewarded for befriending Steph by her mother, who enjoyed spending time with Steph's mother. The mums concocted 'special moments' for the girls and often invited them to spend time together so that they themselves could catch up over a glass of wine. Izzy didn't mind too much as Steph was easy company. Steph listened patiently to Izzy and followed her lead. And Izzy in her turn liked to mother Steph and tell her what to do, because honestly, Steph could be a bit clueless at times, never getting jokes and always saying something random. By Year 6, though, it was becoming a bit boring. Izzy had a lot of other friends in school now and would have preferred to have playdates with Sacha or Sophia, when they could talk about TikTok rather than Harry Potter. But every time Izzy suggested inviting the other girls to play with them,

Steph would become sullen and storm off. It was Izzy who asked if she could go to an independent school, partly so that she could start out afresh without Steph hanging onto her coat tails. At least this way, it wouldn't hurt Steph's feelings and they could 'naturally grow apart'.

Despite knowing that she would be going to her new school alone, Steph had been excited to start as she wanted to learn biology, chemistry and physics. But then there were so many classrooms and the corridors were long and crowded – this was a far cry from her one-form-entry primary school. Steph also struggled socially at her new school. There were too many children jostling about her and she didn't know how to respond to the girls. Izzy had tended to poke her in the ribs when she was meant to laugh. Izzy had also told her what clothes to wear and how to wear them. Now she felt awkward and out of place: she didn't belong. Steph missed Izzy terribly. If Izzy had been there she would have introduced her to the other girls, and they wouldn't snigger at her because Izzy would always make sure of that. 'Steph's cool,' she'd say. Steph wasn't interested in make-up and Justin Bieber like the other girls. They often laughed at things she didn't find funny and although she tried to join in with their laughter, she was aware that she was always a step behind. Sometimes she suspected that she was the butt of the jokes that she didn't get.

Although Steph understood science easily, English lessons were a disaster. Miss Wilding expected her to write three pages describing a willow tree in a storm, when all there was to say was that it was a tree in a storm. The anxiety of asking for help wasn't worth it, she wouldn't know what to say. The noise of everyone talking gave her a headache, and although she tried to breathe normally, she often found she couldn't. So, when one girl pushed her against the locker at school and laughed when she dropped all her books, she had the feeling that if she ever came back to school, she would die.

Feeling like a misfit and an outcast is familiar to many children – but particularly so for children with autism spectrum disorder (ASD). Following a comprehensive autism assessment, this was the diagnosis we gave to Steph. The fact that her condition had not been identified earlier is not unusual. Since autism has traditionally been diagnosed and described in boys, society tends to associate ASD with stereotypically 'male' behaviours and so in girls the condition is often overlooked. Young girls tend to seek approval from parents and teachers, who encourage and reward them for being kind, good, gentle, tolerant and accepting; much more so than their male counterparts. As a consequence, in primary school, many vulnerable and sensitive children prefer to play with girls – who are usually kinder and more forgiving. If a boy shows a preference for playing with girls it is more likely to be remarked upon, and his difficulties (if there are any) may then be picked up by parents and teachers; but no such alarm bell will go off if a girl chooses to play with other girls.* Furthermore, even now, the descriptions of ASD and questionnaires used to assess it are based on symptoms seen in boys. And so, while many parents and teachers will be astute at flagging up little boys who line up their Thomas the Tank Engines, reel off facts about dinosaurs or repetitively spin the wheel of a car, as possibly autistic, they can easily miss fundamentally equivalent female symptoms of ASD – meticulously setting up the furniture and characters of a Sylvanian Family treehouse, for example, or reeling off facts about Harry Potter

---

* Towards adolescence, a complete flip occurs. Social hierarchy in teenage boys has a simple and transparent structure often involving brute strength and athletic and intellectual ability; whereas dominance in teenage girls involves extreme social skill (the dark arts!). Vulnerable teenage girls with autism often prefer the simpler company of boys.

or repetitively brushing the hair of a doll... I wager that many parents and teachers would assume these were appropriate 'girl' activities, as Steph's parents did.

There is another reason why a child's symptoms may not be recognised. As we saw with Ginny earlier, perhaps due to the stigma of mental health issues, psychological and psychiatric explanations are seldom even contemplated as part of an examination of physical health problems.* It is a surprising truth that for many parents the idea of a rare and bizarre infection is often more palatable than accepting a common mental health explanation.** Thankfully, this was not the case with Steph's parents who, following the initial shock and denial, were able to come to terms with the ASD diagnosis, which also helped them to make sense of several 'quirks' that they had already observed and accepted in Steph, and seek appropriate psychological and educational support.

I use Steph's case as an example of peer rejection because it highlights both the explicit and the more subtle examples of exclusion that many people face. Although her difficulty in social understanding (inherent in autism) made her vulnerable to peer rejection, and her reaction to this was more extreme than most, I'm sure that all of us can relate to the experience of not fitting into the 'cool' group, being left behind by a friend or struggling to find our place in a new school. Whether in its most severe form (bullying), or its milder forms (being picked last for a team), peer rejection is an experience that affects

---

* It is also a tragedy that health services are often constructed to prevent dialogue between physicians and psychiatrists (e.g. by the formation of separate mental health trusts) so we all continue to work in our separate silos and do not benefit from mutual expertise.

** PANS/ PANDAS – neuropsychiatric symptoms following infection is a described condition; however, like any other condition, it can be misdiagnosed and over-diagnosed. Therefore, treatment, irrespective of cause, should always include consideration of psychiatric interventions.

children and adults alike; and the shameful negative feelings that it evokes can lead to myriad difficulties in later life.

Swimming against the tide

Even those who have a strong and secure sense of who they are can struggle when faced with the pressure to conform. Resisting peer pressure is stressful and can leave individuals feeling lonely and outcast, and sometimes even lead to real physical and mental danger. Yet this is something that we expect many teenagers to manage alone each day. Ted's story is a good example of the difficulties that many teenagers with antisocial peers face; often being damned if they do, and damned if they don't.

Ted was a 17-year-old boy from Glasgow. He lived with his parents and younger brother Mitch in the rough end of town. On their estate, the boys were tough. Denigrating others, particularly the weaker children, was respected and physical bullying was a part of everyday life. Young people from different estates often congregated in Ted's area searching for trouble and, as Ted looked like an alpha-male type, the lads tried to entice him to join them.

But Ted was different. He took school seriously, wanted to get on in life and enjoyed playing football at a local club. He was sensitive, open-minded and kind, just like his parents. They were tolerant of people from different races, gender and class and had brought their children up this way. Ted was prodigiously talented at football, which was a blessing as it protected him from being bullied; but Ted abhorred violence and the aggression he witnessed on the estate troubled him. His brother Mitch had told him many times that he should just keep his head down and stay out of trouble. But, as Mitch put it, 'My brother can't. He's too good a person – he just can't walk by.' On one occasion, Ted stepped in to protect a weaker boy who was being attacked. He and the boy managed to get away, but the other lads started to whisper and snipe at Ted and soon he became the new target. Ted described a particular blond boy who seemed to be stalking him. He saw him everywhere and felt threatened. One day, Ted saw the blond boy on his own. They got into a fight. Ted broke the boy's nose and fled.

After this incident, Ted experienced heightened fear. Although he enjoyed school, he struggled to get there as he had to walk through the estate. He started to devise more complex routes to school to avoid retaliation from the estate kids, leading to his being late, which resulted in greater anxiety. He worried that the kids might stalk him and hunt him down, so he started to get concerned about leaving traces of himself, 'evidence' such as hair or skin, on seats and tables and he began wiping them down after he stood up.

He was scared of the rage that had momentarily taken over him when he broke the blond boy's nose – he had felt invincible and was worried at the damage that he could have done. Periodically, images of himself breaking the kid's skull against a brick wall flooded his mind, bringing mixed emotions of the joy of revenge and the intense fear of what he could be capable of, because the anger was still burning inside him. He started worrying about what else he could be capable of. The worst thing he could think of was sexual deviance, and he became preoccupied that people were whispering about him being a paedophile. Over time, to stave off his fears, he developed intricate patterns of behaviour which he thought he needed to adhere to to keep safe, for example touching the floor in a particular way and tapping sequences with his feet. Even though he never saw the blond boy again, he stopped playing football. He stopped going to school. He stopped going out. In essence, he stopped living.

By the time I met him, Ted's local Child and Adolescent Mental Health Service had tried in vain to help him and he had been out of school for a year. They had initially ploughed down the wrong path, suspecting paranoia and psychosis, but as the symptoms of compulsive touching emerged, they referred him for specialist assessment and treatment of obsessive-compulsive disorder (OCD).

Anxiety, of which OCD is a manifestation, is one of the most common, but also most treatable mental health conditions. It works something like this: anxiety is an evolutionarily advantageous mechanism designed to alert humans to incoming threats and to prepare us for fight or flight. Our heart rate and respiratory rate increase, our muscles tense and our bowel and bladder empty in readiness for a battle or a sprint so that we can survive. A small amount of this 'excitement' helps our performance: most sports people will 'psych' themselves up before a big game by getting into a 'battle mindset'. But if you have too much anxiety, the emotion is extremely aversive, often crippling performance as a result, and your automatic reaction is to stop the anxiety at all costs. For people who suffer from anxiety, avoidance is the typical escape mechanism: not going on stage for fear of being looked at, not going on an aeroplane for fear of falling out of the sky, not going to the doctor for fear of injections, not walking across an estate for fear of bullies. Somewhere along the way, a chance superstitious thought or action might (temporarily) reduce the anxiety. For Ted, checking that he was not being followed gave some relief. Thankfully, he had not dropped his wallet, which might have allowed the bully to determine his new route to school – but he had better check that he hadn't dropped anything else, a hat, a glove, a hair, a skin cell. This worked in the short term, but each day, the list of things to check got longer and longer. Soon checking was not enough, and the complex touching and tapping rituals that Ted had developed worked to maintain rather than reduce his anxiety and in the long run consumed his life.

Cognitive behavioural therapy (CBT), when combined with exposure and response prevention (ERP), is one of the most effective treatments for anxiety, including OCD.[8] The CBT part teaches patients the theory about anxiety and the connection between thoughts and behaviours. Typically, we envisage thoughts driving behaviour (for example, fear leading to avoidance behaviour); but it is also true that behaviour can increase negative thoughts. For instance, avoiding dogs if you have a dog phobia prevents you from ever learning that dogs can be harmless, which in turn enhances the fear of dogs in your mind, eventually setting up a negative vicious cycle of avoidance. In a similar way, the performance of checking, or any other compulsion, can take the place of avoidance and people eventually become trapped by their obsessions and compulsions.

Unfortunately, for most people, being told how something works never has as much power as experiencing it at work. It's unusual to be able to drive a car competently first time just by studying a car manual or watching a YouTube video of someone driving. You have to get behind the wheel to actually learn. So too with controlling anxiety. The theory is relatively powerless without practice, which is where ERP comes in. This involves exactly what it says on the tin: helping someone to face their fear (by exposing them to it) without them deploying their usual coping response (response prevention) – whether this be avoiding the fear or performing a compulsion. Persuading scared patients to face their fears and supporting them through them is challenging to say the least. Therapists need to be compassionate and trustworthy, but also robustly determined. Some inexperienced therapists can lapse into being 'kind' and allow patients to continue avoiding facing their fears. Therapy in these cases is often ineffective; but who can blame them as there is a natural tendency for caring therapists, like parents, to avoid causing distress? How many of us as caring parents have allowed children not to get straight back on their bikes after a painful tumble? Encouraged children back into the saddle but given up when the child protested and screamed?* We all try to avoid conflict and difficult situations – but it is ERP, the act of facing and overcoming fear itself, that is the curative process. Not all, but a fair number of cycles of CBT for anxiety fail, because of a lack of proper ERP.

For Ted thankfully this didn't happen. After explaining to him the theory behind the connections between anxious thoughts, feelings and behaviour with CBT, we went roaming around the hospital. We left his hair and finger-nail clippings in various different places. It was terrifying for him at first and there was reluctance, protest and resistance. But we took it slowly, and I did not let up even when he was rigid with fear. I stayed with him and talked him through. It took the best part of an hour to get him to gradually retreat from a room where a solitary hair from his head had been laid on a chair. With my support, he at last managed to walk out without removing the hair. He had to look at the hair and know it was there, and he had to leave it there for someone to see, and to experience that NOTHING bad happened. Over the following sessions, we repeated this several times and each

---

* Parental facilitation or accommodation of avoidance of anxiety (e.g. by overprotection and removing obstacles for their children) can serve to maintain and increase anxiety rather than reduce it. The increasing trend for overprotective parenting is likely a contributory factor to increasing rates of childhood anxiety – but that's a whole other parenting book!

time, it got easier and quicker. He felt proud. Finally, building on this momentum, with his consent, I wrote in big letters on the clinic whiteboard 'TED JACOBS IS A PAEDOPHILE' and we had to sit and look at it together, and we had to call staff members to look at it and we had to leave it up in the clinic room while he took his train back home to Glasgow, all the while knowing that some hospital staff in London would connect his name to paedophilia, but at the same time experiencing that NOTHING bad happened. Within weeks, Ted was significantly better. We advised on how his local mental health team could support him and his family, as well as his school, making sure that he felt safe getting there, and within a few weeks he was able to return.

Ted's difficulties arose because staying true to his own values and identity led him into conflict with the values of the peers in his immediate environment. Although he was secure in the knowledge that he belonged in his family, and this perhaps gave him the strength to own his identity, it meant that he was marked out as 'not belonging' on the estate in which he lived. This ultimately became physically dangerous for him and caused his extreme anxiety. Unfortunately, although love and belonging in a strong family unit is desirable and necessary for a child to grow up with a secure sense of self, it is not always enough to protect them against alienation and rejection in the wider world. On a daily basis, many other children and teenagers under the pressure of neighbourhood belonging and the threat of danger fall prey to gangs that cost them not only their identities but their entire futures.

Misfit in medicine

Whereas I had always felt that I belonged in my family, our

immigration when I was a child meant that I didn't always fit in with the environments in which I found myself. I arrived at my new school in 1980s Swansea speaking not a word of English (or Welsh). When I first moved to London, I attended a rough local school for a year and had to dumb down and toughen up to survive. Later, I transferred to a primary school in a wealthy suburban area where I stood out again, this time from my middle-class best friends, due to my repurposed school uniform and the fact that I travelled alone to school on public transport (rather than being picked up by a parent in a car) and didn't have private music lessons. Later still, I felt a misfit in medicine.

As a teenager, I had never wanted to study medicine, art being my best and favourite subject at school. Sadly, I have to admit that rather than having an inner 'calling' to heal the sick, my draw to the profession was a telephone call from aunty number two from Taiwan, gloating about my older cousin's supreme success in his exams. He had aspired to become an engineer but had done so well in his national exams that he had been accepted at the top medical school in Taiwan. This was apparently something that could not be turned down, so my cousin who dreamt of extracting iron from ore went into training to extract infants from orifices. He is now a celebrity obstetrician in Taiwan, bringing into the world the babies of the rich and famous of Taipei. So extreme and prolonged was the adulation for my cousin's genius among the entirety of my mother's extended family that my only response was four words and a grunt: 'Hmpff. I can do that.'

Proving a point is not the noblest reason to enter a career involving years of training and life-or-death situations, but nevertheless it's how mine began. And leaving aside my own arrogance, it was abundantly clear what my family's and school's expectations were: smart children study medicine; the smartest children study medicine at Cambridge University. With hindsight I can see clearly that, even from the outset, my life was about seeking recognition and approval from others.

When I started studying medicine at Cambridge in the mid-1990s, I had little idea what being a doctor really entailed. Although the medical school physiology syllabus was tough and biochemistry was a nightmare, it was during human anatomy, at the trolley-side of the cadaver of a shaved elderly lady, that the reality of what medicine was going to involve dawned on me and I first recognised that perhaps this was not for me. Those early nerves were swallowed down with a dose of bravado, but then I quickly realised that even if one is of a squeamish disposition as I was, it is possible to get through the whole of medical school with little contact with bodily fluids. Partnering with someone who will cut up all the rats and frogs for you and hanging back during human dissection is not that hard when there are plenty of future scalpel-happy surgeons around. Witnessing baby autopsies was unfortunately unavoidable, as was the unspoken pressure to 'toughen up' to the gruesome. Often this entailed distancing ourselves emotionally from what we were actually doing, and it sickens me now to think of it, but 'fascia fights' were de rigueur in anatomy class. These involved the subtle-to-not-so-subtle flicking of dissected tissue at anyone with whom we shared a dissection table. Undoubtedly some of the finest consultants and medical professors in the land started out as immature 18-year-olds picking fights with each other with organs as the weapon of choice. What turned my stomach most, though, was peering into the plastic bins at the end of each dissection trolley and glimpsing a hand, a breast, a lung or what was once the beating heart of a man or woman who had experienced joy, pain, grief and laughter.

This lack of appetite for blood and bile and my 'petty

sentimentality' at viewing bodies as people rather than machinery to fix signalled that my future was not going to be in surgery. Thankfully, within my medical degree, it was mandatory for all students to pursue an additional bachelor's degree to gain deeper insight into an area of chosen interest. An early distinction in a minor psychology exam led me to choose my intercalated BA in experimental psychology. My degree research project consisted of an investigation into the cognitive processes involved in musical mood induction; or rather playing happy and sad music to my mates and seeing how it affected their mood. It was gore-free and even fun. After encouraging my friends to participate on the promise of cake, word quickly got around that I was conducting 'mind-bending psychological experiments' in my room, after which students would emerge elated or desperately miserable. Students started approaching me, offering to participate, and I soon had so many volunteers that I managed to complete my experiments within a week, the fastest completion time on record according to my supervisor.*

Towards the end of medical school, when I suffered a crisis of confidence that I had failed to do enough 'laying-on of hands' during practical sessions, I had to cajole my boyfriend Andrew into letting me practise blood-taking and doing a prostate examination on him. Ouch! There are reasons why some boyfriends become husbands.

But nothing could have prepared me for life as a junior doctor at the turn of the millennium. Newly qualified junior doctors literally lived at the hospital, and this was where we spent every waking moment. Ward rounds officially started at 8am, but could start at 7am, or at any time for that matter,

---

* Should you wish to go on this journey for yourself, the happy music was *Coppelia*, by Delibes, while the sad music was Prokofiev's *Russia under the Mongolian Yoke* slowed down to half of actual speed.

on the whim of our consultant, with the piercing screech of our bleep. If we were on the rota for a weekend, that meant working from 9am Saturday morning straight through until noon on Monday (count it, that's 51 hours straight), and then we were back on the ward as usual for Tuesday 8am. It was actually evidence gathered from the diary exercises of my cohort documenting our 96-hour working weeks that prompted the switch to more reasonable shiftwork patterns for junior doctors.

The only way that we junior doctors survived was through the camaraderie of people bound by shared adversity. I remember Rav, the Etonian pretty boy, more at home in the Stewards' Enclosure at Henley than in the sluice room of a district general, looking shell-shocked when he confessed that the weekend before, he'd admitted a patient but forgotten to put the man on the team's patient list. As a result, the patient had sat in his hospital bed seeing neither hide nor hair of a physician for a week. We all felt for him, as we knew any of us could have made this mistake. I empathised with him further as I suspected that perhaps for him, like me, medicine had been his parents' ambition rather than his own, and he felt as out of place as I did. To make him feel better, I told him about the time that, in a sleep-deprived state, I'd entered the wrong side room to certify a patient dead. As I clicked my pen torch on, readying myself to prise open the corpse's eyelids to check for an absent pupil reflex, the corpse sat bolt upright and bellowed "Allo Doc". I legged it, fearing a zombie apocalypse before realising my own error.

To keep our spirits up, we played tricks on each other. We called each other pretending to be GPs referring in fictitious patients such as Mr Jass, a bloke with a massive anal boil, whose first name was Hugh, just so our colleagues would write up on the big whiteboard of expected patients: Hugh

Jass: Anal boil. Six years of a Cambridge medical education rarely goes to waste.

With time, though, we all developed practical skills of sorts. Patients were no longer traumatised by my repeated attempts to get blood from them. And, although I wimpishly always chose to insert the smallest-gauge male urinary catheter (rubber tube inserted through the penis into the bladder), I became proficient at this too, unlike my gorgeous blond friend Nicola, who always inadvertently gratified her patients in the process: 'The anaesthetic gel is just so slippery!' Following the junior doctor mantra of 'Have a go', I mastered the art of inserting a chest drain and even gained some local celebrity as the queen of arterial blood gas, having succeeded in acquiring a vial of arterial blood where others before had failed.

Perhaps the thought of saving lives should have compelled me to continue my career in physical medicine, but the inhuman hours and relentless workload were getting to me. Certainly, the satisfaction of knowing that your direct actions have led to the survival of others is very potent. I can clearly remember bleeping my registrar repeatedly to come to see 50-year-old Mrs Staunton, whom I had just admitted to the coronary care unit with raging atrial fibrillation. This is an abnormal and dangerously quickened beating of the anterior chambers of the heart, which leads to inefficient blood pumping and is potentially fatal if not treated promptly. 'The SHO [Senior House Officer] and I are held up in A&E,' said my registrar. 'It's mad busy down here. You'll have to do a chemical cardioversion on your own. Just follow the instructions from the textbook.' The nurse brought me the medicine and syringe, and having checked the dosing, I drew it up. Apparently, injecting the patient with this medicine ever so slowly would cure her. I couldn't even look at Mrs Staunton or talk to her, as what could I say? I have no idea what I'm doing, but here goes? As I continued to exert gentle pressure on the syringe, something amazing happened to the numbers on the screen indicating heart rate. First 170, dangerous fibrillation, then slowly but surely the number dropped and Mrs Staunton started to feel and look better. As the rhythm reverted to normal, my consultant walked in. 'You've just saved your first life,' he said, and I beamed inside and out. So I had.

These are the propaganda stories that sell the idea of a career in medicine to swathes of talented youth. What people don't tell you about is the gut-wrenching feeling and perpetual gnawing guilt of not saving a life. It's been over two decades, but I still remember the life I failed to save. It was at the start of another busy night in A&E. I was only a few months qualified but had already gained a reputation for being a grafter. My job as the lowest-order doctor was to be the first to see a patient, take a history and clerk them in. If I saw anyone who looked like they could not last till morning, I had to pester someone senior to review them more urgently. Early on in the shift, a lady from a homeless charity brought in a rough sleeper called Beverley. Although she was in her late sixties, Beverley looked much older. She was quiet and shy, speaking only via the charity worker. The charity worker reported that Beverley was fearful of hospitals and had not wanted to come to A&E at all but had been persuaded to as she had reported abdominal pain for the last six months. Her symptoms of long-standing pain, tiredness and weight loss led me to think that this was perhaps a stomach cancer. After a fairly unremarkable physical examination and checking that her vital signs were stable, I wrote up two bags of fluid and placed her notes in the tray for senior review. The next time I saw Beverley, she was dead.

It was the end of the night shift. I had worked all night clerking in more and more patients. There had been no time to check up on the ones from earlier in the shift. At 8am, the consultant came into A&E to review the haul of new patients. He looked at the patient list and commented that I had surpassed my previous record, having clerked in 11 patients overnight. Before I could congratulate myself on this, the siren sound of the crash bleep went off announcing a cardiac arrest in A&E, right next to where we stood. I ran to the bay, where a team of doctors had descended. To my horror, it was Beverley. The world seemed to move in slow motion for the minutes in which the crash team pumped up and down on Beverley's chest. I willed her to survive, all the while running through her admission symptoms in my head. What had her blood pressure been? What had her blood results shown? What had she told me that I had missed? Why had I not returned to check up on her? When they called the time of death, the leading registrar tutted at the empty bag of saline that hung from the bedside feeding tube that I had sited the night before. The two bags of fluid I had written up as an initial measure until she was reviewed by my senior had long since run through, but it had been so busy that night that no senior had had a chance to review her.

Beverley's autopsy, which I attended, showed that she had died of a perforated peptic ulcer. My colleagues consoled me with the fact that the symptoms of gastric cancer and peptic ulcer are similar, and that many clinicians have made this same mistake. I know rationally that I was not the last person to have seen Beverley alive, but what if I had returned to check up on her? What if the nurses had registered a change in vital signs? What if…

In medical school we were taught many things. About cells, viruses, joints, neurotransmitters, genetics, how to interpret X-rays, MRIs and pathology slides. We were taught how to elicit histories from patients and even how to tell a family their mother is dying. But the one thing medical school didn't teach us about was how to protect ourselves; how to distance ourselves from our patients and how to contain our distress when we inevitably messed up. You learn the former from experience. I am not sure if I have ever learnt the latter. People like me who experience a heightened sense of responsibility and guilt are really not suited for the high-stakes game of medicine.

In the later part of my houseman year – perhaps still rocked by Beverley's death and the sense that I did not want to be responsible for anyone's life or death again – I considered leaving medicine. It was a career choice that had never fully been my own, and I felt that the hospital was not an environment in which I naturally belonged. I wasn't someone who lived for adrenaline, I didn't like making split-second critical decisions, and I certainly had no desire to play God. But just as my houseman year ended, the unexpected opportunity to listen to and understand the life-story of a patient arose and made me consider the possibility of specialising in psychiatry.

Examining the mind as well as the body

Louise Spencer, a well-educated, middle-class mother in her forties, was in pain. She didn't sound as if she was in any discomfort, and when I asked her to move into different positions, she didn't wince in agony or move slowly as one would if they were in pain. Her tummy was soft, not tender, and there was no obvious swelling or redness that would indicate something was severely amiss. When I poked and prodded, there was no protective tensing of the tummy muscles. Still, Louise told me that she had intense pain 'everywhere'.

Many people believe that a doctor's role is to find out what is wrong with them. At some point in medical school, I had realised that, in fact, this was not what doctors train to do. We are trained to find out what is not wrong. We are specifically taught to hold in our minds a catalogue of known medical conditions and to fit the patient's observed and reported symptoms to one of these conditions. If the symptoms do not fit, then by virtue of exclusion, there is either something incredibly rare and very seriously amiss or more likely nothing medically wrong. Louise Spencer was a conundrum because, based on negative blood tests, X-rays, colonoscopies and CT scans, she was going to fit into this latter category. Here she was on her fifth surgical admission of the year, still complaining of immense pain 'everywhere' in her abdomen.

By the time of the consultant's ward round, Louise Spencer's pain had heightened to apoplectic misery. As the consultant prodded her abdomen with his hand, she winced and gasped for air. The surgeons were sharpening their scalpels. Perhaps we should remove part of her bowel and see if that relieves the pain? There was nothing else left to do – she had had every other investigation in the book, and she was still in agony.

At this point, something spurred me to go back to Louise Spencer's notes. I noticed that her prior admissions had all been brief overnighters. She came in with intense pain, underwent a bowel investigation of gradually increasing invasiveness, was given pethidine to help ease the pain and was sent home with co-codamol when negative results were received. Six to eight weeks later, she would present again with the same history.

I decided to perform an experiment. I went to Louise's bedside and told her the truth that, despite finding nothing in any of her investigations, the surgeons were planning to remove her bowel, which may or may not result in her needing a colostomy bag. She looked at me in terror. I asked her if she would rather go home with some painkillers. She said, yes – very much so. She was sure that the pain would be much better if she had her usual shot of pethidine and was sent home with co-codamol. I replied that I would prescribe a different painkiller this time as I thought pethidine and co-codamol (both opiates) were a bit too strong. She was certain that no other painkillers would help and her voice became urgent and desperate. I remarked that, if the pain was so severe that it required pethidine, perhaps she ought to have her bowel removed as the surgeons suggested? 'No!' she exclaimed; she was sure that surgery was not necessary, she just *needed* pethidine'. So began our discussion about her opiate addiction, and I made a referral to the psychiatrists. For me, the listening and the understanding seemed to come more naturally than the poking and prodding. I wondered if this was something I could be good at. I had spent six years at medical school and one year as a physician and surgeon feeling slightly out of place, pursuing the dreams of my parents and schoolteachers, not really knowing what my own dreams were. I hoped that within psychiatry I would find my place of belonging.

Acknowledging a lack of belonging

Like Ginny and Ted, I tried to suppress the misfit feelings I experienced during my medical training, hoping and willing that I would get used to my career choice and learn to fit in. Why make a fuss about not being wholly interested in what I was doing when it meant so much to my parents to have a daughter who was a doctor? For a while, I kept my feelings to myself and carried on, but thankfully I was able to identify that my unhappiness was not sustainable. We only develop the ability to make things better if we acknowledge our feeling that something is not right and become conscious of it; because only then can we contemplate change.

Changing course and growing

Changing course can be difficult to think about because some-times the path we are on is the only one that we know. But continuing down a path that doesn't feel right to you, whether it be a career or a relationship, is not going to make you happy. If thinking about being in the same situation in ten, twenty years' time fills you with dread, you need to pluck up the courage to change course because in the long term, life is for living, not tolerating, and there *will* be a consequence on your mental health.

When we are unhappy, we may not realise it, but our lives begin to shrink. Our social circle, activities, interests and horizons are all diminished, because we are using all our mental energy to tolerate the situation rather than to grow. When a positive change happens, however, we can recover; we begin to grow and branch out, and it is often only then that we realise what a weight has lifted from our shoulders.

If things are not working for you, try doing something different – however small this may be initially, it is a good first step. If you are prone to saying 'yes' and accepting more responsibility, social engagements or work than you'd like, try to say 'no' a few times. On the other hand, if you are always reluctant to try anything new, allow yourself to take on a few more risks and say 'yes' once in a while.

Setting yourself different priorities and applying different parameters to your life is important as this not only allows for new experiences, but also opens the way for new relationships. If something in your life is not working, I would always encourage you to try coming at it from a different angle, and to act unconstrained by a fear of failure or any expectations weighing on you. Ask yourself, if no one was watching, if no one was judging, how would I live my life? It is only by being brave enough to reject what feels wrong that we can find what is right – not just a place where we are tolerated, but a place where we can truly belong.

3

People pleasing: the impact of social pressures and unhealthy relationships

Do you agree with any of these statements?

- It is important for me to be liked and approved of by others.
- I apologise more than I need to.
- I feel I have to be nice to others.
- I find it hard to say 'no'.

If, like me, you found yourself nodding along vigorously, then chances are you are a people pleaser. Or in psychological language, you would score highly in sociotropy tests.

American psychiatrist Aaron Beck described sociotropy as 'a person's investment in positive interchange with others', which basically means that people with this personality type depend on social feedback for gratification and support.[9] In clinic, these patients are easy to spot as they usually minimise their problems and give the answers they think you want to hear, because for them, even the doctor's approval is important. Give them an obtuse question and they often struggle to answer as they can't anticipate what the 'correct' response should be. They want to be 'a good patient'. As an inexperienced junior,

I'm sure that I discharged many such patients, but with experience you recognise that, sometimes, these obliging patients are the ones that are most dangerously on the edge. Research confirms that if people with high sociotropy are exposed to loss of social relationships or stress events that might upset their place in a group, they tend towards increased levels of anxiety, depression, self-harm, chronic pain, eating problems and feelings of hopelessness. A lack of belonging is particularly unbearable for those in this group and because of this, they will try harder than others to conform.

Most of us learn from our parents, teachers and those around us that we have to behave in a certain way in order to fit in. For example, that we should be polite and non-aggressive, that girls should care about appearances and boys should be tough, that supporting Arsenal is fun and that becoming a doctor is a good idea. The evolution of these values, which are commonly shared (except if you're a Spurs fan, perhaps), has clear advantages both for bonding and bringing order to society. One can plainly see how encouraging people to be polite and non-aggressive helps us to maintain social cohesion and peace, but on the reverse side, traditional values seen through modern-day eyes can often appear unhealthy and destructive. For people pleasers, this is particularly dangerous territory.

'You're fat and ugly'

Take, for example, the pursuit of an 'ideal' size and body shape. This is encouraged by societies around the world. It promises membership of a particular group: the 'beautiful' people, and all the good things in life – success, fortune and critically, love – seem incumbent on being accepted by this group. Conversely, 'fat and ugly' translates to 'not good enough' and 'not deserving of love'. This applies to both genders, but particularly to women. Since time immemorial civilisations have evolved to send implicit and explicit messages to women that their role in life is to marry, have babies, nurture families and above all, look beautiful while doing so. The society-wide uptake of these messages has allowed generations of women to be denied education, jobs, suffrage and many other forms of power. It is a sad truth that the success of women throughout history has been to a considerable extent dependent on being physically attractive, and I challenge any woman to say that she has never dressed to please others. Indeed, if the coronavirus lockdown has shown us anything, it is that none of us would choose to wear what we wear to work if not for the sake of others. This applies to men and women alike. But that's where the equality ends, because what women are expected to wear (including heels, make-up and well-kempt hair) requires a lot more expense, pain, time and effort. While there is a growing trend for male CEOs to breeze into work in a sweat-top and shorts, I've yet to see female CEOs in baggy T-shirts and leggings. If a woman stood for prime minister with an unkempt barnet, I doubt that she'd have much success!

While gender equality has made headway in the UK when it comes to voting, education and (most) jobs, the nub of those traditional messages – women need to marry, reproduce, nurture and look good – has been much slower to shift. As a young feminist, I remember being shocked when I realised that the beloved heroines of my youth (Anne and Andie – both with an 'e') were not exactly paragons of feminism: despite supreme intelligence, Anne winds up pregnant seven times while Andie's dreams are fulfilled by looking pretty in a pink dress and kissing a rich boy* – hardly modern-day role models.

---

* Anne of Green Gables created by L.M. Montgomery, and Andie Walsh – Molly Ringwald's character in the 80s movie *Pretty in Pink*.

Although there are now Disney princesses that do more than sing to birds and wait to be kissed; how many wear anything beyond a size 10 or have a raging case of acne? Even today, we continue to focus overwhelmingly on a woman's appearance, hairstyle and clothes rather than on her character, humour or achievements. Undeniably, boys and men suffer some of this bias too, but the extent and degree of it is incomparable. When I think about the impact of a culture that places so much value on conforming to a certain body size, I am always reminded of the time I worked on an eating disorders unit.

The eating disorders unit

Although it was an adult ward, you'd be forgiven for thinking that the eating disorders unit was for adolescents. The bedrooms and communal areas (as decorated by the patients) had a preponderance of the colour pink and 'Forever Friends' duvet sets, and the walls were covered with posters of horses and a fresh-faced Leonardo Di Caprio. There is a psychoanalytical theory that anorexia nervosa is related to fear of the responsibilities of womanhood and a retreat into the innocence of childhood. I wasn't sure about this, but certainly, the décor did seem to bear that out. I had chosen to spend time on this ward because I thought I could readily understand eating disorders: which woman hasn't been on a diet or felt dissatisfied with a part of her body?

How wrong I was. Perhaps it was because the unit I was posted to was particularly renowned, but the cases were extreme, to the point of confounding comprehension. This was circa 20 years ago,* when information about eating

---

* The description of my experiences is based on my memories from 20 years ago and may not reflect current eating disorder understanding and

disorders was not as pervasive as it is now, and many people saw them as 'dieting gone wrong' rather than as severe mental health conditions. For me, it was an awakening. I left with the understanding that the psychological abnormality involved in eating disorders is as serious and impairing as the severest depression or psychosis.

Integration into ward life took some getting used to. Doctors were encouraged to eat with the nurses and patients to foster ward unity and harmony, but although the food was healthy and delicious (Greek salad, Moroccan couscous, fresh fish and vegetables), in stark contrast to the brown stodge being served in other wards and the staff canteen, it was hard to carry this out in practice. There was an intense hum of anxiety among staff and patients alike at mealtimes, with the potential for outbreak into conflict and aggression constantly palpable. On one occasion I heard a piercing, blood-curdling scream coming from the dining hall. I rushed from my desk in fear and wondered if I should call security. When I arrived, I found that the screams were coming from a newly admitted patient who had been presented with a spoonful of hummus that she was required to eat. I learnt that calorie-rich hummus was this patient's particular nightmare – a fear shared by others on the ward. Before patients were allowed to leave the (locked) dining hall, the undersides of all the tables had to be inspected as they would often be plastered with hummus that patients had insisted that they had eaten. This may sound draconian, but calories are the only lifesaving treatment for anorexia nervosa; prior to admission, many women had subsisted on two cherry tomatoes a day.

Neither the nursing staff nor the patients were permitted to leave the dining room until all patients had eaten their

practice. My patient descriptions do not purport to represent all cases of eating disorder and I am not an eating disorder specialist.

allotted food portion, preferably encouraged and supported by their ward mates (thankfully, doctors were exempted from this rule). For new and resistant residents this was tough, and they would dig their heels in, their anorexia telling them that they must not eat. As lunchtime bled into evening with the dining room still in lockdown, there was increasing frustration, and group support could turn into bitter heckling, emotional blackmail and outpourings of vitriol directed at the lone non-conformist refusing to eat. Somehow the nursing staff would need to manage this therapeutically, weighing up the risk that the use of intense peer pressure to get a person to eat might veer into victimisation, with a potential long-term cost to ward dynamics. The eventual consequence, for resistant newbies who continued to hold out, was to be force-fed by tube. The nursing staff who managed these unenviable duties day in and day out were talented, experienced, kind and yet remarkably steely. They had to be, as their work, although at times seemingly brutal, was lifesaving. Anorexia, as I have said, is far from a trivial illness – each and every admitted patient was on the brink of death.

Patients like Eleanor, whose weight was so low when she was admitted that I wondered how it was possible that she was even alive, let alone pacing up and down the corridors. She had already spent a year on a medical ward, where she had repeatedly torn out her naso-gastric feeding tube, eventually severing her nasal septum. The hospital had then plaster-cast both her arms so that she could not pull out the tube any more, since this was the only means of getting food into her to prevent her imminent death. It had been anticipated as a temporary measure, restrictive and shocking as it was, but it had lasted months. Eleanor's disease did not improve and something else needed to be tried.

From this perspective, force-feeding and peer pressure,

although it sounds barbaric, seemed the lesser evil when compared to life in traction or death by starvation. Her condition was so severe that she had been detained under a section of the Mental Health Act,* meaning that she was forced to stay on the ward and participate in treatment against her will, as this was her last hope. By the time I left the ward for my next post, she had gained weight but had moved on to dramatic acts of self-harm, repeatedly slitting her wrists and covering the ward bathrooms with blood. In terms of mental health, hard as it is to believe, this was an improvement. Self-harm of this kind may result in death at some time in the ensuing months or years, but the state of starvation in which Eleanor had first presented would have unquestionably resulted in death in days. These are some of the stark parameters by which we measure improvement at the sharp end of mental healthcare.

NHS digital data shows that in England there are in the realm of 20,000 hospital admissions for eating disorders each year and that the root causes of anorexia nervosa are the same whether weight loss is mild or perilously severe.[10] The desire to be an ideal weight in order to 'belong' is only one facet of the underlying problems, which are inevitably influenced by genes and environment, but many latch onto this superficial idea that a particular weight or body image will be their salvation and will magically make them feel 'accepted' by others and themselves. This is, of course, a fantasy because the real reasons why they feel they do not belong likely run deeper: to feelings of insufficiency, frustration, guilt, anger,

---

* The Mental Health Act is a legal act of Parliament which refers to the care and treatment of people with a mental disorder. Particular sections of the act provide the legal framework by which people with a mental disorder can be detained in hospital and assessed or treated against their wishes. Using the act forms part of the role of a psychiatrist and is often informally referred to as 'sectioning'.

conflict, loneliness, betrayal, self-loathing, powerlessness and ultimately hopelessness and desperation.

This was certainly the case for 19-year-old Sophie. Superficially, one could simplify her case into that of a child actress who had crystallised a belief that being beautiful, and having a certain body type, was essential for success in her chosen career. Her parents had compounded this belief, as her mother had been on the stage in her own youth and had schooled Sophie in the importance of immaculate looks and an obliging smile. Small portions and dieting were often an occupational necessity. At the evening premiere of her first big film, she was offered a designer dress, and starvation to fit into it seemed more than worth it. Rave reviews and interviews followed, where she nailed the surprised-but-delighted reactions, and she sat back and waited for the Hollywood calls to roll in. But the industry is fickle and hard-hearted. The few audition call-backs she received ended in disappointment and she eventually had to return to the sixth form at her old school. One minute the rising star of British film, the next an A-level sociology student. The rejection was hard to bear, and dieting developed into anorexia nervosa.

But digging deeper, it was obvious that Sophie had more profound self-esteem problems. Her parents never seemed to have time to play with her as a child. She remembered a childhood of being polished up and pushed out at her parents' parties in starched frocks to perform a 'cute' set-piece, only to be hastily ushered 'out of the way' to bed once the adoration was over. She quickly learnt that to gain positive parental attention, she needed to be 'grown-up' and obliging – performing when required, invisible when required. For many years, this situation was manageable. She felt 'happy' because she was adept at people pleasing. At this stage, her genetic predisposition to anxiety and depression, via personality traits of high sociotropy and perfectionism, was not a problem as she was in favour.

When her life soured in her teenage years, however, Sophie felt unsupported by her family. They seemed unsympathetic about her rejection by the film industry. Even more problematic, when her parents got divorced and started building new lives, they expected the same 'grown-up', compliant attitude from their daughter that they had instilled in her in her childhood. Her father was filming important documentaries abroad and her mother was spending more and more time with her new partner. 'You know how lonely I've been since your father left me... I really need this.' 'You'll be alright on your own tonight, won't you, Sophie?' Subtle and inadvertent emotional blackmail that people pleasers find hard to withstand.

Emotional unavailability of this kind is highly aversive to people pleasers, whose self-worth is pegged to their value to others, and the combination of high sociotropy and rejection fosters anxiety and depression. Neither Sophie's parents, nor Sophie herself initially, noticed as she became increasingly ill, wearing baggy jumpers to hide her thin frame. Sophie's peers told her she was lucky that her parents didn't care what she did – she could have all the parties, drink all the alcohol and take all the recreational drugs she liked. But she didn't feel lucky – although superficial friendships and short-lived 'good times' seemed like a successful way of coping at the time, in the long term it was detrimental, reinforcing her feeling of a lack of belonging and intimate personal connection. Her emotions, which she didn't fully understand, were overpowering and 'out of control', and she sought to numb them rather than confront them – first with alcohol and then increasingly with starvation.

If she could have dissected her emotions at the time, she would have acknowledged that she felt conflicted towards her parents and towards herself; the conscious desire to please her parents was tinged with an unconscious desire to punish them; she felt hard done-by and yet deserving of reproach – a deadly cocktail of self-pity and self-loathing. When eventually her mother noticed Sophie's protruding shoulder blades and gasped in alarm, Sophie felt secretly warm. Now her mother could see the hurt she'd caused. The family rallied around; her father phoned from Istanbul and professed much concern. 'What's wrong, my precious little one?' he asked. 'Come home?' she pleaded; but his practical response felt to Sophie like another dagger-stab of rejection: 'Yes, of course, my love, in a few weeks – as soon as I'm done with this film.'

To begin with, by restricting her eating, Sophie gained satisfaction from finally being able to take charge of something in her life, exerting supreme control over her body and her family, but before long, her weight loss spiralled beyond her control and even if she had wanted to end the cycle of self-hatred, it had become impossible. Her body, deprived and unaccustomed to nutrients, had shut itself down and become physically repulsed by food, while all the time her emaciated – and therefore malfunctioning – brain told her that what she was doing was not enough, success and fulfilment could still be in her grasp if she could just lose a bit more weight.

By the time I met Sophie, she had severe anorexia nervosa. Like the majority of other young women in inpatient units for eating disorders, her treatment was largely about getting calories in. Our unit only accepted extreme cases of anorexia and most women were admitted with a body mass index (BMI) of around 12 (this is the equivalent of weighing less than 33kg when your height is 164cm). Psychological interventions in people with such low BMIs have been shown to be pointless as the brain is just not working properly. It is only as their body recovers gradually with weight that we can start to consider therapy. For Sophie, who in our one-on-one sessions began to talk to me candidly about her family, family therapy was also felt to be important and yet, confirming Sophie's narrative of emotional neglect, it proved incredibly difficult to get her parents on board due to their conflicting work and social schedules which took priority. I would love to have been able to compare my telling of Sophie's story with that of her parents, as I am sure that they both had their own struggles to relate; but I never got to hear them as they were rarely on the ward. I could only empathise with Sophie, who had battled hard to get her weight back up.

I have learnt over the years that the emotional neglect perpetrated by parents whose emotional availability is limited because of demands from work, health and personal problems, can be just as damaging as that perpetrated by parents whose emotional availability is limited by more conventionally associated adversities such as poverty, alcoholism, drug abuse and domestic violence. The child's experience of inadequacy, worthlessness, shame, broken trust and conflicting emotions of love and hate and the coping strategies that they adopt to try to protect themselves are exactly the same. These children develop a sense of being an afterthought rather than first priority, thus concluding that they are 'not good enough' or 'not deserving of love and attention': in essence not belonging. Often this neglect happens inadvertently and is not necessarily a reflection of 'lack of love'. As mentioned in the previous chapter, as a parent myself, I know that parenting is the hardest job in the world. Having practised adult psychiatry, I also understand that many adults have many and various life problems of their own. Nevertheless, as a child psychiatrist, I can't turn a blind eye to the fact that the way we parent has long-lasting consequences on our children – both positive and negative.

A desire to please others, to be 'perfect' – or at the very least to be agreeable and likeable – is a common trait in many (but of course not all) women with eating disorders. They feel bound to contort themselves to the satisfaction of others, however painful and harmful it may be to them personally; to submit their own needs to the will of others to avoid conflict, or worse, rejection. They can feel that this is necessary or expected of them in order to get along with other people, be it family, friends, partners or employers, and to belong. But being something other than yourself to win approval, constantly needing to be perfect or to forgo your own opinions for the sake of others, takes a great toll on the soul. For how are we able to have a true sense of belonging if internally we are going against, or cancelling, ourselves every day of our lives?

A bird in the hand might not be worth it

For some people, belonging in a group, a family or a romantic relationship, however dysfunctional or unsatisfactory, feels safer than not belonging anywhere at all. So strong is their need to belong, to be wanted, that they become willing to compromise aspects of themselves – their opinions, their needs, their ambitions, their freedom – in order to avoid conflict and continue in relationships. Sometimes the work of the therapist is to help people to see that there is a caveat to the proverb 'A bird in the hand is worth two in the bush' which is: 'but if the bird in your hand is pecking off your arm; it's better to let it go as two hands are better than any bird'.

Toxic masculinity

If women's well-being is adversely affected by the docile bit-part they have been assigned to play in the theatre of life, so the mental health of many men is impaired by the constant burden to be the 'hero'. These may seem like tired stereotypes, but the pressure to conform to these gender standards is deep-rooted in society. For many men, the assumption that they should be the breadwinner, be financially successful, have social status, be more Cobra-Kai than Miyagi-do is extremely damaging. Sometimes life-threateningly so, since what comes with the 'strong' persona that men are encouraged to project in order to belong is a denial of weakness and, critically, a deep reluctance to ask for help. If the men in your life will not even ask for directions when they have taken the wrong route, do you think they are likely to be able to ask for therapy?

Cock fighting

The cultural and societal pressure for men to assert dominance physically or intellectually is very little talked about, perhaps because it is the only way that they have been able to remain in power throughout history. In the ruthless culture of male-dominated professional arenas such as politics, tabloid journalism and academia (and associated twitterspheres), men are actively encouraged to assert their authority by cruelly roasting competitors and adversaries, making great shows of intellectual superiority and indulging in below-the-belt mockery. Just watch parliamentary debates and you'll find that, interspersed between legitimate points, there are pointed personal takedowns. This practice is not only damaging to the environments that dominant men operate in, but also to the dominant men themselves.

Geoffrey, or Professor Simmons as he liked to be known, was a victim of this culture. At 48 years old, his identity was built upon being a successful political academic, a member of the intellectual elite. Critical disparagement of the academically inferior was his forte, always performed with charm and wit. Only latterly, he had backed the wrong horse. His political judgement had been found to be flawed in the most spectacular and public way. Suddenly, it was his turn to fear being mocked and ridiculed by colleagues. And why not? He'd have been first in line himself with a jibe had the roles been reversed. He felt his place of belonging, his standing in polite society, shifting beneath his feet.

The idea that his reputation, and therefore social status, was in decline had triggered severe bipolar depression in Geoffrey. I met him when he was transferred to our inpatient depression unit from the local private psychiatric hospital, where he had spent most of his life savings, to no avail. The nurses and I found his books on Google, where his author biography painted him as an intelligent and charming man. Winchester- and Oxford-educated, Geoffrey told us that he had had a manic episode in his teenage years following the loss of his father, but then nothing until his recent catastrophic collapse, precipitated by his erroneous political judgement. At this point, he was at an all-time low, sleeping all day in a filthy room that he would not let the cleaners touch. He was rude to staff and refused to come out, so I had to consult with him daily in the dark, body-odour-filled room. I knew that his demeanor and situation were affected by his bipolar depression, but having not met him when he was well, I couldn't initially gauge by how much. Often he would not acknowledge my presence; he would refuse to get out of bed, even though he knew that I needed to take his blood each week to monitor his medication levels.

Resolving that we needed to take a different tack, we changed his medication to lithium; so began a gradual transformation that was remarkable to see. Slowly, he started returning to the articulate, dynamic, well-groomed and charismatic man that he had once been. First, he started to sit up in bed in his sodden pyjamas, then he managed to get up and put on his dressing gown. With each passing day, he took increasing care in his appearance, so that soon he was back in a linen suit. With this came the ability to look me in the face and to converse with me – initially this was only about his problems, but later he began asking me about my day and my interests. With the addition of CBT to his treatment, he was able to be discharged to outpatient treatment.

In writing this book, I searched for Professor Simmons online and was saddened to find that he had died in 2013, when only in his fifties. In the years after his inpatient admission, he had divorced his wife, left his family and spent his final years alone abroad. I don't know the part that mental health played in his life after his recovery from depression, but I do know that fully overcoming severe mental health problems is a struggle – and it is an often-overlooked fact that poor mental well-being shortens lives just as physical ill-health does. His obituary described his death as from cancer, but what stood out for me was that it also mentioned 'a brief illness' ten years earlier in his career, omitting to name the bipolar depression that we had treated. The obituary's exclusion of this detail perpetuates the myth that intelligent, successful men do not have mental health problems, an untruth that simply passes the burden of shame onto the next generation of men.

The perfect family

Unfortunately, the ingrained connection between male power and success can be so pervasive that, when some men lose this feeling of dominance and control in their lives, they can become desperate enough to cross many red lines in order to prevent the supposed 'weakness' from destroying them. This sort of desperate male fightback was something I witnessed in the apparently exemplary Pine family.

The Pines were referred to us so that they might participate in a research study, in which we were offering brief telephone psychological treatment to children with mild mental health concerns. They had two children, Ethan aged 13 and Eliza aged nine. Teachers had picked up on Eliza's mild anxiety, thus identifying the family as a possible fit for the study. Her anxiety was below threshold for any referral to local child mental health services but was thought to be suitable for the sort of basic telephone support that we were offering. How wrong we were. During the telephone assessment, it turned out that one reason for Eliza's anxiety was domestic violence in the home. This was whispered by Mrs Pine over the telephone, as her husband was in the next room. I asked if I needed to send the police straight over there, but she insisted this was not required. Mrs Pine confirmed there was no history of violence towards the children. I was acutely aware that this family would need to be referred to social services, and that this process would be easier with the consent of Mr Pine, who I requested to speak to. Mr Pine had been made redundant some five years before. Because of this, he had taken on the role of househusband and his wife had begun to forge a successful career in marketing. In the beginning, Mr Pine had welcomed the break from his job, where he had been overworked and bullied, and had enjoyed spending more time with his children. Over time, though, he had felt taken for granted by his children and emasculated by his successful wife. His loss of power in the marriage affected his identity in the relationship and he began to dwell on the lack of purpose in his life. His loathing of his situation had led to his anger spilling over during ever more frequent arguments, and at times he clearly felt a need to assert his physical power in place of the financial power that he had once wielded. It was as if a noose was tightening around his neck and he needed to fight to break free from it. He wanted to leave his family and domesticity behind, but he couldn't as he was financially dependent on his wife.

Conversely, as Mrs Pine explained, she was reliant on her husband to look after the children as she carved out a career and became the breadwinner. Without his support in the home, she would not be able to continue to work long hours towards promotion. Ethan, the 13-year-old son, was angry at his father's distant parenting, commenting, 'He makes our meals but that's about all he does', and he had started picking physical fights with his dad as well as deliberately flouting his authority in the home. He was increasingly aware that in a couple of years he would be able to square up to his father, take him on and win; and this bolstered his confidence in rebellion. Meanwhile, Eliza struggled to sleep at night and worried that her parents would split up.

Mrs Pine did not want her husband to know that she had disclosed domestic violence, a confidence I was obliged to keep; but after speaking to Mr Pine about his frustrations, I was able to convince him that, given the impact of the unhappy marriage and arguments at home on the children, a referral to social services would be beneficial for the family. Unfortunately, these sorts of referrals are not always successful. When social services contacted Mrs Pine, she told them that she wanted to wait until after the family's summer holidays before leaving her husband. They'd already booked a villa in Mallorca.

After the holidays, social services engaged with the family again, offering support, and the children were given access to counselling. But when I followed up the case with the social worker, she told me that she was not hopeful that Mrs Pine would ever formally report the domestic violence or indeed ever leave her husband. This is the sad reality for many families. They continue to live their lives, hiding their emotions and all the dark things that happen behind closed doors, seeking to conform and convince themselves that everything is fine. I have no doubt that the family and friends of Mr and Mrs Pine assumed that they were the perfect modern family; and many admired the Instagram posts showing a smiling, attractive and well-to-do family holidaying in Mallorca. Sometimes, maintaining the pretence of belonging is easier than acknowledging that something is permanently broken.

The perfect daughter

My parents, like many immigrants, were keen for their children to be financially independent in life. The uncertainty of their immigrant status and the racism they experienced meant that they placed a strong emphasis on concrete demonstrations of ability (academic degrees) and on professions which provided financial stability (in their minds: medicine and engineering). They gave my sisters and me a choice in our A-levels: we could do any of maths, chemistry, biology or physics. Both my sisters took maths, chemistry and physics. I, ever the rebel within the strict parameters set for us, went for maths, chemistry and biology, and also threw in an AS-level in art and design, which I conducted in my own spare time. On the eve of my A-levels, my mother took me to one side and told me in distinct terms that I was their last hope for a child studying at Cambridge, as both older sisters had missed out by a whisker.

I duly applied and went on to study medicine at Cambridge, just as my parents had hoped. On the face of it, I was ticking every 'perfect daughter' box going, but when, at the end of my first year as a doctor, I had to make a decision as to which type of doctor I wanted to train to become, I went against their wishes. I recognised that I could not go on any longer living out my parents' dreams for me in general medicine and I took the decision to enter psychiatry.

Many people get confused about what a psychiatrist is, so let me explain. Psychiatry is a medical speciality (paediatrics, neurology and gastroenterology are other examples of medical specialities) requiring a primary medical degree. Training in psychiatry follows the same pattern of training and on-call responsibilities as other medical specialities: you have at least 6–8 years' training as a junior doctor, which is split into Core Training (this was called Senior House Officer years in my day) and Speciality Training (or Specialist Registrar training in old money). Only once this training is complete (requiring the passing of many, many exams) are doctors referred to as 'senior doctors': that is, consultants or associate specialists. As consultant posts are limited, and highly competitive, many doctors spend additional time as a junior doctor doing research to improve their chances of becoming a consultant – meaning that many junior doctors, including those who have embarked on specialist training in anything from neurology or surgery to psychiatry, may still be junior doctors well into their thirties, with families to support, and are in fact not very 'junior' at all! When I chose to enter psychiatry, I had in mind becoming a bit like Robin Williams in *Good Will Hunting*: a cardigan-wearing doctor, giving sage advice in the form of psychological therapy to troubled youths in a clinic resembling a Victorian living room rather than a ward.* But it quickly became evident that this was not going to be the reality.

If my early medical years had been tough, my initial experiences in psychiatry were even harder. While medical on-calls were often predictable (largely chest pain and shortness of breath), in psychiatry you could never anticipate what would happen next. A friend's first on-call involved a fully naked gentleman being dropped off at the emergency clinic by a black cab; one of my own early challenges involved having to evacuate a locked ward in a fire – not easy when many independent-minded patients actively sought death or had other priorities to avoiding it.

Half the patients we saw were desperate souls who were self-harming and overdosing, and who wanted to be admitted. We had to turn many of them away. The other half we had to haul in on mental health section against their will. They were often intent on fighting their way out. Like the life-or-death decisions of medical on-calls, psychiatric on-calls involved sometimes impossible choices, as we tried to ensure we turned no one away who really needed to be admitted, while at the same time having to act as gate-keepers for scarce mental health beds: 'Is this patient going to significantly hurt or kill themself tonight if I let them walk out?' or 'Is this patient going to hurt someone else tonight if I let them leave?'. Despite

---

* Psychiatrists are sometimes confused with clinical psychologists as, often, the role of the psychiatrist and psychologist overlap. Both psychiatrists and psychologists are trained in psychological interventions/ psychotherapy, but only psychiatrists are medically trained and therefore able to prescribe medication.

our best efforts to help everyone, we often had to give patients and families news that they did not want to hear. I vividly remember one such event, involving Liz and her brother Jack.

Jack had brought Liz to A&E after finding her semi-unconscious in a filthy flat, lying in a pool of her own urine. It turned out Liz had relapsed following discharge from an alcohol detox programme two weeks earlier. I had to deliver the news that we could not offer Liz a bed. She had been blind drunk, but there was no immediate mental health problem to admit her for, and there was no way that the alcohol service would be readmitting her any time soon, given that she had only recently received the full treatment with little effect. The only thing I could do was let the alcohol service know that she had relapsed – they would be in touch to offer outpatient support. But Jack was not having this. How could I say there was nothing I could do? How could I expect him to take her back home to her filthy flat? She was clearly unwell. I felt a lot of sympathy for him, but I also had a job to do and a line to toe. My specialist registrar had been clear: 'She can't be admitted.' Jack leapt at me, pushing over hospital para-phernalia and screaming obscenities at me. Liz, for her part, tried to intervene to help: 'Leave off, Jack, it's not her fault, I did this to myself.' I pushed the panic button. Two security guards came and dragged Jack out of A&E, his screams of 'You f***ing bitch, I'm going to get you for this...' echoing down the hallway, and the malevolent look in his eye dead-locked on me. I held it together enough to apologise to Liz and leave, but when the A&E consultant asked me if I was OK, I couldn't stop shaking and collapsed in tears. My bleep went off – there were more patients to see. I wiped my tears and gritted my teeth. 'I'm fine,' I said to the A&E consultant, and back I went. My only thought was that, for once, I was glad of my impossible-to-remember-and-spell name. Jack would be unlikely to be able to look me up and follow through on his threat.

For me, the saving grace during my psychiatry training were the friends I made along the way. Seventeen other junior doctors started the journey with me – all of whom initially seemed somehow more prepared and robust than me. They say that psychiatrists generally fall into two camps: those interested in 'psychoses' (schizophrenia, bipolar disorder), and those into 'neuroses' (anxiety and depression). I was clearly in the neuroses camp – it turned out that I was just as scared of conflict and aggression as I had been of blood and bile.

Although I lacked clinical experience when I started, I had conducted some epidemiological research work on teenage mental health in Cape Town, South Africa, on a secondment after my house jobs. As part of the survey, my team of students handed out questionnaires at various schools across the Western Cape, from the poorest township (where the headmaster's office was riddled with bullet holes), to the fanciest Afrikaner private school (where the headmaster's office was encased in Italian marble). This was over two decades ago, and the country, not long post-apartheid, was still plagued by violence and gross inequality. It was a breeding ground for post-traumatic stress disorder and mental health problems in general. The data I collected would contribute to the development of a national schools' mental health programme, which, in a country like South Africa with limited mental health resources, was felt to be the most economical way to combat mental health problems in children. While I was in Cape Town, a friend's cousin took his own life with a bullet in the mouth at Rhode's Memorial. This prompted me to look at data on suicides in South Africa, which as I had suspected, showed a spike in young, white, male deaths, reflecting not just international data, but possibly also a degree of white guilt in the South African context.* A paper I wrote at that time was awarded a research prize. I was shaken by this young man's death, and the cohort of young male lives that he represented that were being lost internationally, but I was pleased that at least my research was making an impact.

Buoyed by this experience, I sought to specialise in adolescent depression. I initiated a meeting with the head of the Child Psychiatry Faculty, Professor Townsend, to pursue this area of study. Following his advice, I contacted a brilliant female lecturer in the Psychology Department and began working with her on behavioural genetics in teenage depression. She gave me access to her dataset on twins with adolescent depression and I set to work on analysis, learning new statistical tools. Under her guidance, I published two papers in high-impact peer-reviewed journals, and with my existing papers from South Africa, went on to become a clinical lecturer at my university at the age of 29, which wasn't bad going. I was elated to see my name in print for the first time and felt proud that my hard work had counted for something. I felt at home in academic psychiatry.

Indeed, the academic training programme was my sanctuary. I loved the intellectual stimulation of the lectures and the discussions with my fellow trainees. It was like university again, only better, as for once I was interested in everything I was being shown and I knew that the information I was garnering could be put into practice to the benefit of my patients straight away. We were taught about the theory of psychiatry: the mind, the brain, how drugs and psychological therapies work, the importance of genetics, but also how

---

* White guilt in this context refers to white people feeling personally responsible for their adverse life outcomes despite privilege (rather than having an external source of blame such as a discriminatory society, which is protective for suicide).

environment and life experience can change gene expression and brain development. That it is not all nature or nurture, but a complex interplay of the two.

After a hard day's graft, we junior psychiatrists would gather in the Sun and Doves and talk about the week's mishaps and interesting things that had happened. Our mentors, junior doctors a year or two our senior, would give us advice that we would lap up. There was Amelia, already working for a knighted professor; Priya, the President of the Junior Doctors' Committee (JDOC); and Irish Johnny, the gregarious JDOC events organiser. They were our spirit guides while we found our feet.

Now that I was finally pursuing something that I had felt drawn to personally, not only did I enjoy the act of day-to-day learning, working, researching and teaching, but I was surrounded by like-minded people: people with a strong social conscience, with one leg in the science camp and the other in the arts. It felt as if I'd finally found my tribe and the world was my oyster.

Less happy were my parents, who tried for many years to persuade me to change course to paediatrics or neurology. This, I later learnt, was a very common experience for psychiatrists. Psychiatry is seen by many doctors as rather second rate – in fact, psychiatrists are often considered 'not real doctors'. So strong is the stigma of mental health that not only do patients lose out time and time again on service funding,* but so too do the doctors trying to help in terms of research funding,** and crucially there is no parity of esteem. I soon realised that my

---

* Since 2012/13, funding for mental health trusts has increased by just 5.6%, compared to an increase of 16.8% for acute hospitals.

** Just 5.8% of the health research budget is spent on mental health research. This amounts to £9.75 spent per person affected by mental illness compared to £1,571 per patient for cancer research.

parents were too ashamed to tell their peers that their much-boasted-about Cambridge-educated daughter had ended up in psychiatry. When they imagined my career as a doctor they had dreamt of clean clinics and sterilised theatres, not police cells and locked wards. They told their friends that I had become a neurologist!

It wasn't until many years later, towards the end of my specialist training when I decided to specialise in neuropsychiatry, that my parents came around to accepting my professional choice. At least they could now say I was a neuropsychiatrist, because adding 'neuro' to the front of any word adds kudos (neurosurgeon – way sexier than a bog-standard surgeon, and neuroanatomy – sounds much cleverer than anatomy, doesn't it?). Maybe they could also now see that I was finally enjoying my career and understood that I wasn't going to change track, despite their urgings. Whatever their reasons, it felt good to finally hear them tell their friends what I really did. I felt glad to be back in the fold, and at the same time somewhat taken aback to realise that, even as a fully-grown adult, my people-pleasing desire to be 'the perfect daughter' was still at the beating heart of me.

Recognising people-pleasing tendencies

If you identify as a people pleaser, then you have taken the first step to improving your well-being. Begin to think about what you are doing in the various areas of your life: is it for yourself or for someone else? Do you want to study law or medicine? Do you want to wear those sky-high heels? Do you want that hand on your ass? Do you want to stay at work late? Do you want to 'take one for the team'? Do you want to marry and have children?

If you are doing things to please a parent, friend or partner, you shouldn't be afraid to point this out. A loving parent or partner who is concerned about your welfare may not even be aware that they are influencing you in any way and they will probably appreciate the feedback. At least once they know, they can try to see things from your point of view and accommodate mutual change or negotiate a compromise. If the love and concern part is not there in the relationship, then you need to re-evaluate it (see 'Removing toxicity' later on in this chapter).

Giving yourself permission to say 'no'

We all have to be selfless and do things for other people at times, but it's important to be aware that this is what we are doing and not lose sight of our own needs and our self-worth. It is never OK to be taken for granted or taken advantage of. Sometimes this means saying 'no' to the unfair demands of others, which may cause upset; but remember that doing things we are not comfortable with to make others happy is to the detriment of our well-being; it's also a hindrance to true belonging. Saying 'no' may mean confronting our own fears of failure or of being alone, but ultimately, it can lead to self-respect and even the discovery that we are stronger and more resilient than we thought.

Supporting people pleasers

People pleasers can be difficult to spot because, by virtue of wanting to please others, they often don't say when they disagree and just go along with things. As family, friends and employers of people pleasers, we all need to be aware of our contribution to their mental well-being. Just because these people are willing to do things to please us (that fourth A-level, having sex on demand, giving up their job, staying at work late) doesn't mean that we should ask them to do these things, and it doesn't mean that we should let them. My husband is frequently suggesting weekends away, on the assumption that my mother can take care of our children. My mother is a doting grandma and always says 'yes' if I ask, but it is my responsibility not to ask unless I really need to, and I take this responsibility seriously.

Parents of people pleasers: be wary of endorsing overachievement as this often fuels people pleasing rather than curtailing it. Parents need to be aware that children, however talented, are not immune to burn-out – in fact, they are more vulnerable as they are less able to gauge their limits or control their environment. It is part of parental responsibility to ensure that children do not push themselves too far and to reinforce the need for balance and priority setting rather than overachievement.

Partners of people pleasers are often happy to have a compliant spouse and do not contest the status quo. In their defence, they may say, 'I never knew they were unhappy. If they weren't happy to have sex/look after the children/give up their job/do the domestic chores, then they would have said, wouldn't they?' Likewise, employers of people-pleasing staff are often all too happy to engage in 'voluntary exploitation'. But partners and employers need to understand that it is hard for the people pleaser, who is frequently in the weaker position in a relationship, to speak up or make demands. Their lack of active protest does not equate to consent but rather reflects deep-rooted powerlessness and fear. I would therefore implore partners and employers to consider the balances of power and burden and to address this without being asked.

'If you admire an eagle, why would you put it in a cage?' This is the question I would like to ask many men I know, but dare not do so. They sought to marry incredibly intelligent, high-flying women who kicked ass in the boardroom. But then, having been attracted to this type of woman, they have been seemingly content to see or even actively encourage their wives to give up their jobs to be stay-at-home mothers.

The parody of the 'desperate housewife' stoked up on anti-depressants or painkillers is not so funny in reality, as I learnt from Louise Spencer. Some eagles are happy to be domesticated, but I know many that would like to fly high and free and are prevented from doing so by a desire to please their husband, by their feeling of maternal duty (as imposed by society) and by their need to belong in a family.

Likewise, I should say, many men are pushed hard by status-driven wives to provide more, reducing many dedicated dads to drab salarymen.* Situations like this are breeding grounds for poor mental health – not only in the case of the desperate housewives and office workers but in that of the children they are raising.

Similarly, anyone who holds the balance of power in the workplace needs to take care to nurture good relationships with their colleagues and employees. Many bosses worry that a reprioritisation towards well-being in an occupational setting is a slippery slope towards lack of ambition and reduced productivity, but this is not true. The most successful people in business will know that in all walks of life, relationships are everything: happy staff are loyal and more productive, happy clients keep coming back and generate further business and a happy family life allows staff to thrive at work.

Prioritising meaningful relationships

In our world today, we can all too easily be consumed by the hamster wheel of work, money, achievement, competition, prizes and status. Yet what has got me through the hard times in my life has always been my relationships with people around me. If you were to ask anyone on their death bed what meant most to them in their lives, they would talk about the people they have loved.

* A similar situation occurs in same-sex couples or couples where traditional gender roles are reversed, whereupon the 'male' role refers to the person with greater financial power, irrespective of gender.

People in the Twin Towers and Grenfell Tower, with the knowledge of their imminent death, called their loved ones. I doubt anyone rushed to email their PowerPoint presentation to their boss or check their bank account. If relationships are our priorities when we have one minute to live, why aren't they when time is on our side? Many of us need to value our relationships more.

This means not only nurturing relationships with people that matter to you and support you, but also recognising the ones that are unhealthy. Ensure that you are able to be your true self in your friendships, as superficial friends can be burdensome. If you feel you need to act in a certain way that is uncomfortable and are unable to voice your true feelings to friends, you may need to consider whether these friendships are worth investing in. In addition, friendships should be mutual: if you find that the support you offer others is never reciprocated, consider whether or not you could voice this. If you feel unable to speak honestly, then again assess the relationship priority. On the other hand, if you find that you gain immense support from your circle of friends and it seems that your friends have no problems at all, think about whether you are exploiting them. It may feel good to be the centre of attention and support all the time, but really, exploitation never works well in the long term. Part of the joy in relationships and life in general is in giving to others, and a sense of belonging is as much about the giving as the taking. You cannot expect to feel accepted and supported if you do not accept or support others. Likewise, if you feel you are constantly judged by those around you, think about whether you yourself have a tendency to be judgemental, as the two frequently go hand in hand.

Parents and siblings

Sooner or later, much as we loathe to imagine it, our once idolised and invincible parents will become decrepit and in need of care, and all too soon they are gone from our lives. The coronavirus pandemic has made the fragility of life clear for all too many of us. Make the most of these family relationships while you can and try to remove the possibility of future regret.

Removing toxicity

Unfortunately, not all relationships are positive, and recognising when one is unhealthy – be it with a family member, partner or friend – is critically important. To help you to do this, imagine what your life would look like in five and ten years' time if nothing changes, and write a letter to yourself from the future. What would you advise yourself to do? This is a technique borrowed from motivational enhancement therapy, which helps hone the mind to think about whether change is needed and what the potential negative consequences of 'doing nothing' are. If we have recognised the need to change, we must be brave enough to chart another course. This takes a lot of courage – a leap into the unknown is frightening. But it can be made easier if we have other, more positive relationships and support behind us, giving us the reassurance that we will be able to cope, survive and thrive again. Part of the fear of leaving something behind is the myth of no return, but of course, although we never feel it at the time, paths can be retrodden. Keeping bridges open where we can is important. If a relationship is not working, it may be time to leave, but there is never a need to mistreat or humiliate others in the process. Making our needs known, being honest while treating others with respect, humanity and in a way that we would wish to be treated ourselves is always a better option, as it allows us a route back if we make wrong decisions. Life is about opportunity, and the more bridges we build and leave open, the more opportunities we create for ourselves.

4

Loneliness: isolation and feeling alone in a crowd

Psycho-gerries

During my training, no place better exemplified the consequences of loneliness than the services for 'Mental Health of Older Adults'. No one ever called it that then, of course. It was always politically incorrectly referred to as 'psycho-gerries'. Looking back, it is easy to be shocked by the use of such derogatory terms, which were widely used. I mention it here, because I think it is important to remind ourselves how far we have come in the last 20 years in terms of modifying our language to connote compassion for rather than ridicule of those with mental health problems. The Mental Health of Older Adults ward on which I was sent to work was instantly familiar to me, as I had spent some work-experience time in my school days running an art club in a care home. The date, including critically the year, was written in massive letters on the whiteboard every morning and staff would speak at TWICE THE USUAL VOLUME at all times. My ward served an area with a large African-Caribbean community, and most of the nursing staff were African-Caribbean too, meaning that it had its own unique vibe. The wafting music of Vera Lynn would float out of the speakers one minute, and the reggae beats of Bob Marley the next; waltzing would alternate with soulful hip swaying and rhythmic stamping. Bring-and-share lunches featured goat stews and rice and peas with a side of plantain. Regular ward activities still always included Bingo and a nostalgia group (this consisted of the same discussion every day as participants would forget they'd participated and said exactly the same thing the day before) and my favourite days were when the hairdresser would come and make everyone look and feel a million dollars. This pampering and social interaction was all the more important as, from talking with my patients, it was clear that for some time prior to their admission, many had been socially isolated; and this had contributed to their mental ill-health.

My septuagenarian patient Douglas had had severe clinical depression since his retirement – to the extent that he would not eat or drink, which was now beginning to compromise his physical health. His depression was associated with delusional feelings of morphological body change. A psychoanalyst could interpret these symptoms as a manifestation of his sense of estrangement and lack of belonging: he felt alien and had become convinced that his body was morphing and changing so that he no longer fitted into a normal human environment. His main concern, and the focus of his severe depression, was the absolute belief that with each passing day, his arms were getting longer and his legs were getting shorter. I had never encountered these symptoms before and coined it 'Mr Tickle syndrome'. Each time I saw Douglas, he professed his arms were now too long to manage. He claimed that his arms could sweep the ceiling while he sat on the bed and that if he stretched them out wide, he would be able to touch the walls on both sides of his bedroom, despite both of these things being observably untrue. He claimed that his legs were so short now that they could not reach the ground, all the while with his plaid-slippered feet firmly planted on the hospital linoleum. He gave no explanation as to why this was happening to him, but said he could not go on like this. At least he admitted to feeling depressed and was willing to accept treatment. 'Wouldn't you be depressed if this was happening to you?' he'd say.

Many people who have this feeling of not belonging say that it is not something they have experienced throughout their lives; it has developed through circumstance and grown over time. Unlike people who have always felt out of place, for those who lose their sense of belonging, there is the added resentment of the cause of the loss and a painful memory and yearning for what once was. Prior to the Covid-19 pandemic, this most commonly occurred in old age, a time when health, independence, purpose, family and friends gradually and cruelly drift away. But over the last year, with social distancing and quarantining becoming widespread and prolonged, most of us will have had first-hand experience of social isolation and will be able to recognise the negative emotions that this generates.

For Joy, her memories of her glamorous, action-packed younger days must have hurt when juxtaposed with the circumstances of her later years, living alone in a bedsit in Brixton. Joy was a 75-year-old, tall, slender African-Caribbean woman. Her face was always expertly made up behind her massive, thick-lensed glasses, but perhaps the most striking thing about her was the blue plastic carrier bag that she wore on her head. Joy told me about various suspicious goings-on in her bedsit; she said people had been drinking the liquor miniatures that she collected and moving things around. Initially, she had blamed her pesky nieces who came by every month, ostensibly to check up on her, but really, she knew, just to get their hands on what little money she had left. Latterly though, she had seen shadows in the night, heard male voices talking and worst of all, they had tampered with her when she slept, so that now, they could steal the thoughts straight from her brain due to the metal plate they had implanted in her head. She rapped at her forehead in confirmation. 'Hear that sound? That's it right there – the clunk of a metal implant.' She believed that the thought transmission was impaired by plastic, hence the blue bag on her head.

Although talking to Joy about recent events was filled with the nonsensical and the bizarre, hearing about her youth was fascinating. She showed me a photograph of eight Caribbean beauties in revealing silk gowns and four-inch heels encircling a young, up-and-coming British celebrity in a top hat and tails. She pointed out one woman in particular, and to my amazement, the facial features were unmistakably hers. She had once been Miss Caribbean, and, for a while, had led a champagne lifestyle, sailing on yachts and attending the most glamorous of parties. She had married the man in the photo 'who was just a boy then – look at him', but the relationship had not lasted when he became famous.

Joy's trajectory from the dazzling world of her youth to her tiny flat in Brixton clearly showed a dramatic change in lifestyle, and I wondered how this may have affected her identity and mental health. Declining beauty and declining opportunity had culminated in social isolation, leading to alcoholism and paranoia. I considered the role of that one photograph, over 50 years old, that she had brought with her and clung to: her heyday and her life-long love. I noted that she had kept her husband's surname and how, while he had since married twice, she had remained single.

Our job was to help Joy rebuild her life. We started by

making the plastic bag redundant by 'removing' the metal plate from her forehead. This was done in a matter of weeks, not with surgery, but with a highly effective anti-psychotic medication. As she recovered, we contacted the 'pesky nieces', who were actually grandnieces in their early twenties, Joy's only remaining family. They visited her on the ward. 'We want to help you, Aunty,' they said solemnly, 'but you never let us' – to which Joy, now rid of paranoia, nodded in response, with tears in her eyes. 'Yes, I could do with help.' The occupational therapist accompanied Joy to her bedsit and cleaned it up. The empty liquor miniatures, which Joy had secretly overindulged in, were removed in a blue plastic carrier bag.

Loneliness is not the same as solitude or choosing to spend time in our own company. It is about a disconnect between our desired quantity and quality of social interaction and what we actually achieve. It can occur at any age and can happen to any of us. The negative impact of loneliness on people is hard to overstate; it is known to be associated with physical and mental illnesses, including blood pressure issues, poor sleep, dementia, depression, suicidal ideation and even premature death. A 2010 study of the impact of loneliness on death rates estimated its effect to be double that of obesity and quadruple that of air pollution, making it a key emerging public health concern. It is estimated that in the West, a third of people are affected by loneliness, with 1 in 12 severely affected.[11]

Scientists have also been studying how the experience of loneliness can affect our psychology and have found that it causes changes in measurable brain structure (differences in grey and white matter). Given that the brain is the primary organ for making sense of our environment and controlling our bodily responses, this should perhaps come as no surprise. It just goes to show the powerful effect of the environment, and crucially our interpretation of the environment, on our mental and physical well-being.[12]

Alone in a crowd

Social isolation, however, is not the sole cause of loneliness, and many can feel lonely even when surrounded by others. Scientists used to measure loneliness by monitoring the extent of people's social contact and group membership, but they now know that quantity matters less than quality.[13] It is more about how well you identify with a group than the number of groups you belong to, or the number of social interactions. You may, for example, be a member of the school football/basketball team, while your real passion is for singing and dancing (think of the characters in *Glee* or *High School Musical*). You may be part of a heterosexual couple and loving family unit but be gay (a recent example being the TV presenter Philip Scofield). Perhaps you feel like you know lots of people but are not really known by anyone. Recognising that you are not being your true or full self with those around you can lead to a lonely existence, fuelling mental health problems.

Behind the smiling mask

Maude was a patient from my Mental Health of the Elderly outpatient clinic. She was a colourful character, an outspoken Jewish grandma who sashayed into my cramped little clinic room like royalty. With her purple-rinse hair, large bright-yellow Perspex spectacles and vibrant-green dangly earrings with matching eyeshadow, she was difficult to miss. Maude was vital, confident and alive, in contrast to many of the other elderly patients, and I wondered why she needed to be in clinic at all. Here was an elderly lady with oomph; who was thriving, not just surviving. 'What's brought you to clinic today, Maude?' I asked, genuinely puzzled. 'Well, doctor,' she said in all seriousness, 'it's my vagina.' For emphasis, she made the hand motions I associate with the opening line of 'Twinkle, Twinkle Little Star' and uttered theatrically, 'It's going "bling, bling".'

When I took the rest of Maude's history, there did not seem to be any other manifestation of illness, mental or physical. She lived alone; but had a busy social life within the Jewish community. A woman in her seventies who was maintaining her appearance with make-up and jewellery, and actively socialising, was living well in my opinion. I could imagine her making cheeky innuendos, shocking her few remaining male contemporaries at synagogue and intrusively taking over at local charity fundraisers. I presumed this was her character, and why not? If there was ever a time when you could feel free to speak your mind, it was at her age. Perhaps her vaginal symptoms were more 'burn, burn' than 'bling, bling' and were indicative of yeast infection, so I asked her to have it checked out by her GP, but made a follow-up appointment just in case.

At the follow-up, other symptoms started to reveal themselves. Although Maude's vagina was no better, she was no longer concerned about that. She had started a new social activity: exotic dancing. Before I knew it, Maude had hitched up her gypsy skirt and was demonstrating her new skills to me in my clinic room. Swinging her hips and undulating her belly, I had to admit this was a bit out of the ordinary, even in a psychiatric clinic. As she cornered me against the filing cabinet, I blamed only myself for my predicament: for having missed an evolving mania. The situation would have been funny if it were not so impossibly sad.

'I'm worried about Maude from my outpatients,' I told my consultant the next day. 'Either she has always been extremely eccentric and inappropriate, or she is becoming manic.' As I divulged the history, my consultant got onto the phone with the team occupational therapist. They arranged a home visit for a few days later. It was just as well, for as the euphoria of mania buoys, the comedown of depression sucks out life. Maude's flat was in unhygienic disarray; she had obviously not been coping for many, many months: piled-up dirty dishes, a soiled bed and empty fridge. The occupational therapist had caught Maude rummaging through her neighbours' bins looking for food – a rather diminished figure compared to the larger-than-life character I had described to the team. Gone were the earrings, make-up and colourful clothes. Gone was the animation and overt sexuality. Here was the real Maude stripped bare: an old lady who had clearly had no visitors to her home for months; who went out to do charity work but felt unable to ask for charity; whose green eyeshadow and funky jewellery hid the pain of abject loneliness.

Maude was surrounded by people most of the time and proactively sought social interaction. But the majority of Maude's social life was superficial. It would have been difficult for passing acquaintances to realise that she was actually desperately lonely. What Maude lacked was close friends and family nearby, people that might have dropped by to see her in her home, to check up on her and to notice how she was really doing. We treated Maude for bipolar disorder, a condition that had likely first emerged mildly in her twenties but had gone undiagnosed, her husband Frank having supported her lovingly for many decades. Over the ten years since Frank's death, Maude had tried to keep herself on an even keel, but it was difficult without him, the stable rock who had kept her grounded, and her moods had become increasingly erratic. She had become incapable of managing the day-to-day tasks of paying bills, buying groceries and doing housework, and this self-neglect had compounded her mood difficulties. On recovery, together with social care, we moved Maude into sheltered accommodation. Here she could remain active, independent and sociable, but there would always be someone on hand to keep an eye in case her vagina went 'bling, bling' again.

Teen isolation

Second only to the elderly, teens are well known to suffer loneliness and isolation. Adolescence is a time when identity creation is to the fore, when experimenting with self-expression through peer connection and competing for social hierarchy are important rites of passage. The downside of competition for social hierarchy is of course that bullying, and more recently cyber-bullying, is highly prevalent and a well-known contributor to loneliness.

A literature review on social isolation and loneliness in teenagers during lockdown showed increased risks of depression and anxiety among this group, prompting fears that there will be a massive increase in demand for already stretched child mental health services in the aftermath of Covid-19.[14] Indeed, my own Tourette's service has already seen a doubling in referral rates for teenage girls, many of whom are presenting with unusual 'tics' (the making of involuntary movements and sounds), which can be both florid and exaggerated. These tics are not like the movements associated with Tourette's syndrome, and are more likely to be functional tic-like actions. Remember that functional symptoms can be generated by psychological triggers such as anxiety? Ginny, whose case I described in Chapter 1, developed functional seizures and paralysis due to her fears of academic failure, and Steph, in Chapter 2, experienced functional regression due to social anxiety. One consequence of the stress of Covid-19 in 2020, and the social isolation and educational uncertainty that arose from school closures, was that many susceptible teenagers, especially girls, developed functional tics or tic-like attacks. An added notable observation was that some had the exact same tics displayed by Tourette's influencers on social media platforms.

There is concern that social media sites such as TikTok may have had a part to play in this phenomenon. These sites have exploded in popularity – and videos of influencers with tic-like symptoms have gone viral. For example, the hashtag #tourettes on TikTok has 2.5 billion views, with numbers doubling in the month of January 2021 alone. Although teens report that they gain peer support and recognition from this exposure, this 'support' may also be inadvertently reinforcing and maintaining symptoms, as well as opening the door to the potential for 'contagion' among vulnerable individuals.[15]

Parents and commentators are understandably concerned about the potential impact of social media on children's mental health, questioning whether this form of interaction could damage their real-life social ability, by reducing the amount of face-to-face contact they have with others and stunting their communication and empathy skills, thereby fuelling social isolation and loneliness.

These are important issues to consider, with depression and anxiety levels in children having risen over the past decade – i.e. even prior to Covid.[16] But, as ever, the picture is more complicated than it looks at first glance. A growing body of evidence suggests that social media use is not detrimental to children in and of itself – indeed, the use of social media has been linked to mental health benefits as well as problems.

Rather, social media is a mood reflector or enhancer, and while happy children with good self-esteem may gain support and positivity from it, those with low self-esteem and low mood may use it in a way that is detrimental to their mental health. Evidence to support this includes Chloe Berryman's 2018 study on this topic, which found that adolescents who lack confidence and are prone to making comparisons between themselves and peers on social media are more susceptible to depression; whereas teens who are able to present themselves authentically are more likely to have well-being benefits from social media use.[17] Her study found no direct associations between hours online and loneliness, but revealed that good parent–child relationships and social support were protective factors. My take-home message from this research was that we need to have more awareness at a granular level about the ways in which vulnerable teenagers are using social media. Certainly, children who feel rejected by the world can be drawn into online communities which seem to offer them a sense of belonging – and which may or may not have their best interests at heart. Some websites can raise awareness of mental health problems, while others promote unhelpful depictions for entertainment purposes; equally, some support groups empower members to live fully and recover, while for others membership and 'belonging' is dependent on them maintaining their illness. Sadly, there are even some online groups that hook vulnerable young people in with the promise of belonging, only to encourage self-harm, starvation and in some cases suicide and murder.

Loneliness is, of course, not the preserve of teens and the elderly. Working-age adults can certainly experience it too, although research is limited for this group. One of my favourite books of recent times is Gail Honeyman's *Eleanor Oliphant is Completely Fine*, which so astutely observes and describes stark loneliness in a young adult.[18] The story hit home as it drew my mind back to a colleague of mine from my days as a junior psychiatrist.

When I knew him, Johnny was a larger-than-life, buoyant character in charge of running social events for junior doctors at the psychiatric hospital. For a year or so, he would join us at the Sun and Doves – the pub where we would all gather after a hard day's work. Pint in hand, he'd tell us stories with a unique dry wit. As we all moved on to different specialist training programmes, however, Johnny went into adult psychiatry and I never saw him again. A few years later, during my specialist training in child psychiatry, I received an email from the hospital inviting colleagues to his funeral. For me, 20-something-year-olds were not supposed to die, especially not 20-something-year-olds that I knew. I called Priya, who I thought would have stayed in touch with Johnny, as they had moved to adult psychiatry together, and asked her what had happened. She hadn't been in touch with Johnny for some time, but she'd heard the word on the street: that Johnny had died by suicide.

Johnny had been struggling for some time with personal life events and had developed drug and alcohol problems. A patient had complained about him, leading to his suspension and a General Medical Council inquiry into his fitness to practise. A few weeks later, neighbours had found him hanging in his flat. I knew that mental health problems were complicated and multifactorial. I understood that I hadn't really known Johnny beyond the bright and enthusiastic trainee socialising in the pub, when he had given us advice and organised splendid parties; but to me it felt deeply shocking – as if 'one of our own' had been taken. Someone very peripheral perhaps, but someone who was there during a formative time in my life who I just presumed would 'always be there'. Thinking back to those evenings in the Sun and Doves, I wondered: was the extroversion, friendliness and extravagance genuine or was it a projection of who he thought he should be? Was he already having mood and drinking problems then (we'd always met in the pub, so it was natural to be drinking)? Why was Priya not in touch with him any more? Had anyone been in touch with him? Had he always felt alone in our crowd?

What shocked and devastated me too was the fact that he was a psychiatrist. We worked for the same mental health trust. I struggled to understand how a service that looked after the mental health of millions was unable to identify problems in its own staff and help them. Was there no one at work with whom Johnny had felt able to talk about his issues before they got so dire? We advised our patients to seek help from their families, schools and employers and yet it seemed we didn't foster a culture in our own organisation that might facilitate this. Would my organisation look out for me if I fell?

Identity crisis

A part of me understood Maude's and Johnny's feelings of loneliness despite their having active social lives. A funny thing happened when I arrived at Cambridge in the mid-90s. As soon as I got there, many staff and students commented on my good English. Initially, I took great offence at this: how else did they think I got into Cambridge, if I couldn't grasp the language? Later, I realised that in my college undergraduate intake of 120 that year, I was the only BME girl who was not a foreign student. Everyone just presumed that I was a foreign student and were hence surprised at my flawless accent. Russell Group universities routinely bumped up their atrocious record on BME admissions by admitting fee-paying foreign BME students. These same 'cash cows' who aided the university's BME stats were paraded in all its promotional material. One of my best friends, a mixed-race foreign student who was the only 'black' student in my college year, always made it front and centre in the college prospectus. If you looked carefully at Cambridge's promotional literature of the time, you'd find the same handful of black students in every shot!

According to the statistics for the period covering my time at Cambridge, when university education in the UK was still free, 50% of home students (UK nationals) came from state schools, 40% were female and 5% were ethnic minority.19 If you do the back-of-an-envelope maths, this made me one of the 1% of home university students who was a BME, state-school-educated female; or to really put this in perspective, I was one of the 30 such students in the entire year at the university – roughly equating, as I found in reality, to one per college. As such, I felt a little different from my peers, and it was frequently an uncomfortable place to be. For example, on various occasions, I was accused of being a 'quota filler' – a cheap jibe from the threatened. I knew that my grades matched those of my privately educated white male peers, however, and I graduated with the same grades as the majority of them.

Thankfully, in my day, there were no tuition fees. Even so, although my parents were now earning good salaries, I was still eligible for means-tested hardship funds at Cambridge. I took these as well as student loans. Although I did not work in term time (which is forbidden at Cambridge due to the rigour of the courses), I worked full-time every Christmas and summer holiday, initially at a dry cleaners, and then, realising that I had more potential than this, as a medical secretary (it helped that I could spell diarrhoea and ankylosing spondylitis). This helped with my living costs and afforded me the extravagance of May Balls and backpacking holidays in interesting places such as Budapest, Bucharest, New York, San Francisco and Cape Town.

But there was no set 'clique' that I could comfortably blend into. The drinking societies were filled with white blonds, the Chinese societies were full of Crazy Rich Asians, and when on one occasion someone did reach out and invite me to a party, it turned out they were trying to convert me to Christianity. When I was elected to my college student executive, I realised that not only was my demographic a minority, so too were my views. My one vote in favour of giving college money to the university LBG (now LBGTQ+) society was shouted down by the other nine students on the committee because 'there were no gays at our college'. My citing of statistics showing that LBG students represented some 10% of our population at that time led to searching looks from the ten exec members around the table: 'You mean – one of us is gay?' I kid you not. Unfortunately, against this backdrop, my lone voice, which I had not yet learnt to use as I so wanted to belong, was drowned out and the motion did not pass. The money was given to the student bar.

In search of my own tribe, I spent my time at Cambridge joining everything from the Chinese societies, the Black and Asian Caucus and the Cambridge Union (posh debating society, membership of which cost a mere £100), the Cambridge Student Union (CUSU, where I later became part of the women's executive championing gender equality), to the *Cambridge Arts Magazine*, the pottery society, college rowing, football, netball and badminton. I made a lot of friends in different places, but it wasn't until one May Week in June that I realised that I was replicating my early school history of shapeshifting: changing myself to fit in. I had been invited to four parties that fell on the same day: the Patricians' male drinking society garden party kicked off at 10am, the feminist gal pals were congregating at the CUSU garden party at noon, the Blacks and Asians were barbecuing to steel drums at 4pm and I was attending a party with my friend Andrew at the Pitt Club (Cambridge's equivalent of the Oxford Bullingdon, a private club known for its wealthy members, grand dinners and bad behaviour) till late. In between each event, I had to leg it home because 'the look' required for each event was distinctly different. I faced the ludicrous scenario of changing from Cotswold's wedding attire to plaid shirt and DMs to batik sarong to heels and a mini-skirt. I realised then that belonging everywhere really meant belonging nowhere; but I didn't know how else to be.

In many ways, Andrew became my ticket to belonging at Cambridge and things started to fall into place after we met in my fourth year. He was a postgraduate foreign student from South Africa. Blond, six foot two and privately educated, he could have been a cast member of *Riot Club*. He had no problems fitting in and within months he was not only friends with people who belonged to the Pitt Club, but had also joined the Hawks' Club and acquired a Cambridge Blue. His friends were cut from the same cloth. They had establishment credentials and the establishment welcomed them.

What had attracted Andrew to me – a five-foot-two Chinese state-educated immigrant? Andrew's rugby-playing Australian friend Chris didn't understand our relationship at all and was taken aback when Andrew introduced me to him as his girlfriend. I was familiar with this sentiment as in my first three years at Cambridge I'd already become used to rejection. Interracial relationships were certainly complicated there at that time. I had felt on a few occasions that some boys that I was close to were unwilling to cross the line into a relationship with me because of our racial difference and how that might look to others.* I certainly wasn't someone to be brought home to meet the parents.

But Andrew and I recognised ourselves in each other. Andrew told me of his feelings of loneliness among friends in South Africa, where the culture highly values sports over history, art and reading and where, because of his appearance, he was taken for 'a jock' every time. To all intents and purposes, he hid his interests and opinions and was never fully himself in South Africa, but playing a part. Our backgrounds, although culturally different, had the same core values of education and a love of children – by coincidence both our grandfathers had been primary school headmasters. But just like me, while he had had many friends, he had never had a best friend, because neither of us had ever been 'ourselves'. Being from South Africa, he was acutely aware of the existence of social inequality and the damage structural racism can wreak. When Andrew was 14 years old, his father had taken him to meet Nelson Mandela, before he became the South African president. These experiences meant that, when I questioned racial slights, he validated me rather than cancelled me as everyone else did, even my closest friends. Strip aside our very different exteriors and our internal parts were the same. Through me, he accessed the arts and ethnic and social equality scenes that had eluded him because of his establishment credentials, and through him, I accessed the establishment. We became each other's best friend.

---

* I was open to relationships with men of my own ethnicity of course, it was just that there were so few British Chinese at Cambridge. The few of us there tended to avoid eye contact with each other in case we'd be automatically bundled together by virtue of race. My parents were predisposed to a Taiwanese match for their daughters and indeed my eldest sister had been subjected to a parade of Taiwanese PhD students whom my mother deemed a 'good match'; but thankfully my parents gave up the cause for all of us when she married a Frenchman.

When Andrew finished his studies at Cambridge, he had to return to South Africa and we faced a long-term separation. It was a difficult time for me. Although his intention had always been to come back to the UK, he struggled to secure a visa. The long-distance relationship was tough; we spent every holiday together either in London or Johannesburg; and when that got boring, we'd meet at an airport in Delhi or Jakarta. We phoned and faxed each other (this was the pre-Zoom and peak fax era) on a regular basis, and my wallet was full of those newsagent scratch cards for making cheap international calls. Although I had my friends and family, there was no denying that at this time I was often incredibly lonely. Flying back to London from a far-flung airport was awful and I always felt sorry for the passengers who sat next to me on those flights, as I usually cried for the whole journey – and it wasn't the gentle trickle-of-tears-down-the-cheek kind of weeping, but gasping, snorting uncontrollable sobbing. Not knowing exactly when you will see someone you love again, wondering if love will survive or whether your loved one will wander is hard to bear, but I clenched my jaw and carried on. It was probably because Andrew was not around for three long years that I was able to work gruelling hours and dedicate my life to psychiatry. I ate, lived and breathed it.

Later on in my life, loneliness reared its ugly head again – this time during maternity leave. During antenatal classes, mothers-to-be are given a wealth of information about pregnancy and birth, but it surprised me how little advice we were given on how to parent children or maintain our own well-being. We mothers were prepared for morning sickness and torn perineums, we were talked through the pain levels of labour, and perhaps there was a brisk mention of 'baby blues', but no one ever mentioned to me that early motherhood could be so intensely lonely. The subject is rather taboo, as women with babies are considered blessed. Having children and a family is the 'ultimate goal of all women' and so this should have been the nidus of my self-actualisation.[20] And yet, some of my loneliest moments were at this time – crying on the floor alongside a crying baby. Much research has been done into the symptoms of postnatal depression, but more action is needed to spot social isolation and loneliness in mothers of young children more generally, to prevent this progressing to more serious mental health problems.

Seeking out others

If meaningful relationships are the essence of life, then the more we have, the fuller our lives and the hardier and more resilient we become to life's adversities. Evidence backs this up, as studies show that having a wide network of social ties and good personal support helps people withstand higher levels of stress. But even if we have generally been quite successful at maintaining good, supportive friendships, things can change, and at some point in our lives, perhaps through a house or job move, we may find ourselves needing to establish new relationships. One way in which we can make this potentially daunting prospect much easier is by changing our mindset so that, instead of being afraid of rejection, we start to view everyone as a possible friend.

When we look back at our lives, making friends in nursery and reception seemed so much easier than at any other subsequent time. This is often because very young children have not yet developed the hang-ups, insecurity and negativity that life inevitably generates in us. We saw everyone in our nursery class as a possible playmate, we behaved naturally with the assumption that other people would like us. For most people, making friends in nursery was a matter of playing together and smiling.

If we see everyone as a potential friend, rather than worrying that they or we are the 'wrong' race/intellectual level/social class etc., then making friends becomes a lot easier. Look for things that others have in common with you, rather than focusing on differences, and you'll soon realise that there are many more people that you can relate to than you thought. The less we judge or make assumptions about others, the less likely we are to feel judged. By being open-minded, we can often be surprised to find that people who appear superficially different are more like-minded than we imagined. Without this attitude, I would never have got to know my husband Andrew, for as someone politically incorrectly put it to me, we were superficially different: 'How come you two are a couple? You have slitty eyes and he has round eyes.' I should have replied, 'Because the shape of our eyes is irrelevant; we have the same hearts and minds', but unfortunately the best comebacks are always the ones you think of days after the moment has passed.

When I had problems at work, it was largely the compassion of my colleagues that helped me through, as they were the most likely to understand the particular nuances of my experience. I also discovered a wonderful social media group called Physician Mums Group UK, formed of some 20,000 doctors who were also mothers. The support I obtained from this virtual bunch of strangers was literally lifesaving (the access to instant medical advice was an added bonus). So you can see that, despite the bad press of social media, it also has myriad benefits. If you have a problem, it's very likely that someone out there on the internet has been through something similar and is willing to offer support.

Caring for carers

If there has been one thing that the coronavirus pandemic has shed light on it has been the hard work and critical role of carers in our society. This group can include parents caring for disabled children, children and adults caring for parents, or a spouse/partner caring for their other half. Care work can make one particularly vulnerable to loneliness as it is usually a physically demanding, never-ending and thankless task. On top of this, caring often involves the painful daily reminder of what has been lost, whether it be in a loved one's mind, spirit or physical ability.

In the 1990s, social care in the UK evolved from being institutional to community-based. I think this was positive, as given a choice, most older people would prefer to remain engaged in their own communities and stay in their own homes for as long as possible. However, without the political will and funding, good ideas can turn into nightmares, and nowadays, the burden of care of the elderly and disabled in society can all too often fall on unsupported families. Indeed, current social policies covertly depend upon informal home care by relatives, and the needs of these unpaid carers, who contribute so much to society at their own expense, are largely ignored.[21]

On this issue, my thoughts return to the boy in the cage and how our society is perhaps getting closer to that sort of last-resort coping strategy than I had ever imagined it could, as families are left without expertise, resources or support, to care for their loved ones as best they can. Given that we all hope to get old someday, we need to ensure that carers are sufficiently financially and emotionally supported, not least so that they do not fall prey to loneliness and mental health problems of their own.

If you are a carer and relate to some of the feelings I have described, try and set aside some regular time for yourself to do something for your own well-being, whether this be an outing with a friend or a trip to the cinema. Organisations such as carersuk. org can provide support and guidance.

PART TWO

Why we struggle to connect

5

Brain wiring: neurodiversity and neurodevelopmental disorder

During the Covid lockdown, we all learnt more about ourselves and our families. One thing I learnt was that, while I was happy to sit tight indoors a week at a time in front of my computer by day and Netflix by night, my husband would *need* to go out (fully masked of course), at least once a day. Running or making visits to the Tesco Express to buy one or two items at a time was his solace. I found a similar variation among my patients, all of whom I now saw virtually. Children who hated the social aspects of school were thoroughly enjoying being at home, as their symptoms of anxiety remitted, while others were in desperate tears about being parted from their friends. The truth is that although connecting with others is a basic human need, how much we need to connect and how good we are at doing so varies greatly from person to person.

Think back to your last office Christmas party. You'll be able to pick out the social elites, commanding centre stage and working the room. You'll also be able to pick out a few 'wallflowers', standing at the side-lines, nursing a drink. And then there will be the less visible ones, those smoking outside, or hiding in the toilet, or at home with a feigned illness. So in-built is social ability that if you go to a four-year-old's birthday party (with two children I've been to a fair few of these), you can spot exactly the same characters – the kids who gather around the birthday boy, eagerly taking part in games and activities, and then the other little ones, those sat on their parents' knees, those crying under the table in the next room, those examining the wall socket or the ones who were intentionally uninvited or forgotten.

Those who are less socially attuned often experience the world in a different way, their brains are wired differently and they are less aware of social norms. The drive to conform to social norms is genetically built into most of us, to the extent that we often don't even realise that we are doing it. Even as young children most of us learn quickly to copy others when we don't know what to do and agree with others sometimes even when in our hearts we disagree. We somehow know to do this, even without being explicitly told to. Classic experiments conducted in the early to mid-20th century by the psychologists Muzafer Sherif, Solomon Asch and Arthur Jenness demonstrated that we are all susceptible to 'group-think', no matter how independent-minded we believe ourselves to be.[22] They performed experiments on conformity in which individuals were asked their opinion on an arbitrary task, for example estimating the number of beans in a jar or the length of a line. Afterwards participants were exposed to contrary group opinion and surveyed again and, in most cases, they revised their own views to be more in line with the group one. However, there are always some who are less susceptible to this group-think mentality, those who don't recognise the sense or purpose of conformity. These individuals may be more attuned to things that others are unaware of (sounds, smells, background details), while remaining ignorant of the things most people find fundamental.

On the one hand, being a non-conformist is an admirable

position and can be positive (for instance it can make you less vulnerable to peer pressure, more likely to be able to focus on personal goals and objectives without being swayed by others), but on balance, in a society which rewards those who are socially able, non-conformists can find themselves feeling different, abnormal or outcast. As if they don't belong.

Dispelling myths around autism

Some people who struggle in this area may be surprised to find that, if tested, they would meet the modern criteria for autism spectrum disorder (ASD). New definitions of ASD and its uncoupling from intellectual disability have led to recognised prevalence rates as high as 1 in 60. There are plenty of people at the top universities and in high-profile jobs who would likely meet diagnostic criteria for ASD.[23]

People with ASD can have different needs from other people. Sounds and smells that many of us are accustomed to, for example, may be overwhelming for people with ASD. They may need more routine and less emotional stimulation than others and find it more difficult to read social cues and express emotions. Much as some people fear that a vaccine or rare infection is responsible for ASD, the reality is that its pathology is far closer to home. Of all mental health problems, autism has the most genetic contribution, with some twin studies finding around 90% concordance in genetically identical twins.[*][24]

---

* Concordance rates refer to how likely twins with the same genetic make-up will each develop the same disorder. By contrast, other mental health problems, such as depression, have an identical twin concordance rate of about 50%, suggesting a much larger role of environment or life experience than in autism. ASD is also highly prevalent in many known genetic disorders and increasing numbers of

Moderate and severe forms of ASD, and ASD associated with intellectual disability and lack of language, are usually picked up in infancy by paediatricians; but milder forms of ASD, or ASD in those with preserved intellect, are often not noticed in early life and these individuals can end up being referred to adolescent or adult psychiatry with emotional and behavioural problems. This is because the demands of relationships and the complexity of unwritten social rules increase exponentially from adolescence to adulthood, causing confusion and distress. For instance, no one actually tells you explicitly whether a glance from another person is a 'come hither' or 'get lost' look – most of us can intrinsically 'just tell' the difference between them; but what if your radar for this, and many other social cues, was 'off'? It can lead to all sorts of awkward misunderstandings and a heap of stress. People who struggle in these ways can, despite their best efforts, become aware that they are getting it wrong, and the sheer effort of trying to conform to a confusing landscape, constantly policing and editing their own behaviour, eventually takes a toll on their mental health and can result in anxiety or depression.

This was what happened to Krish, whose difficulty only came to light following a minor incident, at the age of 14, during a conflict with his father. His teachers had no inkling of his problems. From their point of view, he was well behaved and appeared to be 'happy' at school with his two close friends. In truth, the teachers had their hands full with other pupils and anyone who got on with their work and didn't come to them to volunteer their worries was considered 'happy'. Krish had known for some time that he and his friends were the 'socially rejected' and they were routinely ridiculed by the lads on the rugby team. He had become accustomed to being shoved into

small genetic anomalies are being found to be linked with ASD.

the lockers for no reason and being the butt of jokes. As a result, he had become indifferent to his peers at school, even his friends. He thought them childish and inconsequential.

Krish's parents had had concerns about his social interaction for some time. They noted that he had problems relating to others but, as this had never caused major problems, they had not thought to pursue the issue. This was just Krish, the son they loved. From a young age, he took apart his toys rather than playing with them and would form intricate geometric figures with fridge magnets. They noted these 'quirks' were unusual – his sister didn't have them – but again, they were not causing problems. They figured that these qualities were a feature of his high intelligence. His tested IQ was 149, so he coasted through primary school with only a brief period of mild anger outbursts.

But recently, Krish had started to fixate on the feeling that school was a waste of time and his objection to attending had increased to the point where it was a physical battle to get him to go. His family were alarmed, but were struggling to get their voices heard as Krish had an intellectual comeback for everything. They said that school was good for him socially, but he felt that relating to others 'was a bit unnecessary'. His academic-sounding arguments wore them down. Krish maintained that he wanted to study politics and had ample internet resources from which to pursue these interests at home without a need for school. He spent most of his spare time researching this area to degree level and felt the subjects he was forced to study at school were 'pointless'.

Then one day Krish had a bad argument with his father, which started when his 11-year-old sister had refused to come off the PlayStation when it was his turn. Krish had wrenched her off it, throwing her across the living room with force. According to Krish, his father had yelled at him 'ferociously' without even listening to his 'perfectly valid explanation': that he had requested she come off the PlayStation and had even told her what he would do if she did not. In Krish's mind, given that his sister had chosen not to comply, she deserved the outcome. He felt that his father had acted unfairly towards him, not for the first time. This latest row compounded his growing feelings that he was always treated unfairly in his family, because although they operated on a policy of 'democracy'; his parents and sister all thought in the same way (valuing movie night and family get-togethers, which he found boring and intensely painful). His opinion never counted for anything, as in any vote, he lost. Despite good abilities and competence in some areas, there were clearly other aspects of understanding that Krish found almost impenetrable.

Krish had stormed off after his father had scolded him, ostensibly to calm down, but when his father went outside to check on him, he found Krish had passed out, having attempted to hang himself from a pear tree in the garden with his school tie. At which point, everything changed. When Krish disclosed longstanding feelings of having wanted to 'vanish from society' and described himself as being 'redundant', his family rallied around and supported him. Krish said that he had been 'going through the motions' most of his life, that there did not seem to be any purpose to anything. He was seen by his local child mental health team, who identified depression and the need for an autism assessment.

Twenty years ago, Krish would not have been diagnosed with autism, and perhaps even today, his symptoms could be missed by services that are not used to seeing children with autism and high intellect. His presentation would have been described as depression alone. He would likely have been treated and have recovered but continued to have a sense that he was different, unlikable, 'wrong' and perhaps continued to blame himself for 'not belonging'. Despite his high IQ, in the real world, he would probably have struggled to function.

Traditionally, autism was thought to be related to intellectual disability. The terms Asperger's syndrome and high-functioning autism were introduced to describe autistic symptoms in people with preserved intellect, but in more recent times, we have come to understand that they are versions of the same condition. The availability of big data and GWAS (genome-wide-association studies) has facilitated much research into the genetics of autism and revealed that the genetic basis of the condition is more complex and the spectrum of symptoms far wider than once thought. The terms Asperger's syndrome and high-functioning autism are now retired, given that it is recognised that autism can affect people with any level of intelligence.* Furthermore, we now know that some of the characteristic features of milder forms of autism can confer a genetic advantage: a propensity to follow rules and routines, an ability to focus on details and sustain attention on specific interests, a preference for rational actions rather than knee-jerk emotional responses. To get rather un-PC about it, there are often times when Sherlock Holmes is preferable to the proverbial damsel in distress. Nevertheless,

---

* The fact remains that there are more people with an ASD diagnosis that have low IQ, as a diagnosis is usually only sought and made if the person is impaired by their symptoms in their daily life. There are likely many people with average to high IQ who would meet criteria for ASD; however, a diagnosis is neither sought nor made because of lack of impairment. These people are able to use their IQ to learn to conform and adapt to their symptoms. For these people in particular, the 'neurodiversity' descriptor is helpful and valid to them for making sense of mild day-to-day difficulties that they experience but which do not substantially impair their occupation, well-being, relationships and self-esteem. Incidentally, most people with an old diagnosis of high-functioning autism have IQ in the average rather than superior range, yet another reason why these misleading terms have been made redundant.

when a threshold of symptom variety and severity is reached that starts to impair a person's ability to function in day-to-day life (for example generating overwhelming anxiety and low mood), clinical diagnosis for autism should be sought, not least to help their self-awareness and prevent them from succumbing to additional mental health disorders.

It was necessary to look at Krish's depression in the context of his autism in order to treat it more effectively, because what he needed more than an anti-depressant was to understand himself and be understood by others; he needed to belong or at least understand and accept why he didn't. The autism diagnosis enabled Krish's family and school to understand that, despite his intelligence, Krish had weaknesses in certain areas that required support and understanding. That for him, adapting to the family's and society's routine was hard work and that for all his life it had required huge effort to bend and conform to others, often resulting in frustration. So that a person with autism is not left to try and maintain this constant one-sided compromise, we encourage discussions between them and their family and school to promote mutual understanding – there has to be concession from both sides to find a way forward for everyone. Most importantly, for Krish, his diagnosis gave him an explanation for why he was the way he was. Rather than being 'redundant', 'wrong' or a 'misfit', he had discovered that there was a scientific explanation for his condition; and there were many other people like him, who thought in the same way, and had the same strengths and the same struggles. Although Krish definitely needed support to improve his mood, his new self-awareness and his family's acceptance of him for who he was could finally allow him to belong – a critical starting point for improvement in his outlook on life.

ASD is an example of different brain development,

which doctors (lovers of long words) commonly refer to as neurodevelopmental disorder. The other common neurodevelopmental disorder is attention-deficit hyperactivity disorder (ADHD), which describes people who struggle more than most to sustain concentration (inattention), tend to act without thinking (impulsivity) and find it very challenging to stay still (overactivity). Both ASD and ADHD arise from different brain wiring – typically because of distinctive genetic make-up or environmental insults during brain formation in utero and early infancy (for example prenatal exposure to alcohol, physical injury during birth). While 35 years ago, when I was a child, diagnosis of children with neurodevelopmental problems was somewhat rare, these days it is commonplace. ADHD prevalence rates are around 5–7% (1 in 20), and as mentioned earlier, ASD occurs in 1 person in every 60, meaning that there is likely to be at least one child with ASD and/or ADHD in every school class in the land.[25] Although most children with moderate-to-severe autism and/or ADHD may find life challenging, and in their case the label of neurodevelopmental disorder is appropriate, more recently, people with mild ADHD or ASD and intelligence within the average-to-high range have expressed a preference for the notion of 'neurodiversity'. This more empowering and normalising terminology is a more accurate reflection of their experience, in that, as mentioned above, mild ASD and ADHD in people with good intellect can also confer benefits, and could be viewed as part of normal brain variation. Human genetics and personalities are diverse; and aren't we glad they are! Life would be terribly dull if we were all the same. Wouldn't it be even better, though, if society could come to accept a person with a weakness in social ability and attention as readily as they can someone who is asthmatic or short-sighted?

Understanding inattention

Just like autism, ADHD can impact on a person's social interactions and therefore their ability to feel that they belong.
People with ADHD often forget social engagements, become
impatient when listening to others or say or do things without
stopping to consider if they may be wise or hurtful. This
happens no matter how hard they try not to. These actions can
upset others and cause frustration and exasperation, leading to
recrimination: 'Why did you do that? What the hell is wrong
with you?' Over time, these comments become internalised to
'There's something wrong with me', making people feel like
outsiders and leaving them with a profound sense that they are
'naughty', 'bad' or just 'wrong' in some way.

Between training as a psychiatrist and specialising in child
psychiatry, I worked for several years on a medication trial of
stimulants for children with learning difficulty and ADHD.

Back then, there were strong negative preconceptions
about ADHD: that the condition was due to 'bad parenting',
'lazy teachers' and was 'not a real disorder'. Some people
even suggested it was a label fabricated by doctors in order
to medicate difficult children because – 'it didn't exist in
my day'. People who think this way – and some still do –
have likely never spent much time with a child with full-on
ADHD. With my cautious clinical hat on, like many other
people at that time, I myself had concerns about medicating
children, but I was aware that my opinions were based on gut
instinct rather than fact and I was open to working on a drug
trial to see for myself the costs and benefits.

The basis of a (take a breath here!) gold standard double-
blind randomised, placebo-controlled trial is that the doctor
– me in this case – is not told whether the 'medication' doled
out is a drug or a cornstarch pill. Parents and children are

also left in the dark. Hence the 'double-blind'. At the time it was already well known that stimulant medication (methylphenidate in this case, an amphetamine) was highly effective in treating ADHD in children. However, most large clinical trials had actively excluded children with an intellectual disability, despite the fact that children in the intellectual disability range were more likely to have ADHD. Our study sought to rectify this by only accepting children to the study with tested intelligence in the mild-to-moderate learning difficulty range.

I probably felt as gangster as a Chinese nerd ever will as I travelled around the south of England from Canterbury to Southampton, with large bottles of pharmacy-grade amphetamines in my bum bag (or cornstarch of course!). I dutifully assessed each child I treated for improvement and side effects and was fascinated at the end of each case when I was 'unblinded' – allowed to find out which medication my patients had been taking. Those who had been prescribed stimulants undoubtedly benefitted more.[26] But it was also interesting to see that the act of taking a pill was able to bias parents and teachers into seeing an improvement in most cases even if the pill was made of only cornstarch; and, equally, how the families with a child on placebo regularly reported amphetamine side effects that had no biological basis. It's no wonder that many people report benefits from homeopathy and other 'non-evidence-based medications' or can feel physically ill from consuming gluten* (or other media-maligned food groups). Ultimately, it is this power of the mind over the body that is at the heart of why I find psychiatry so fascinating. One of my most memorable patients at that time was Mark.

---

* People with coeliac disease and confirmed allergy exempted.

The impact of correct medication

Mark and his dad came to my ADHD trial clinic on the south coast from the local trailer park. Mark senior was extremely thin with a few missing teeth, while Mark junior was his exact opposite. When I asked after his mother, he bellowed, 'A *beast*. She is *a beast*!' I wondered if this was some kind of a joke. 'OK, but why does that mean she can't bring you to clinic?' I asked. He sighed at my evident stupidity. Mark senior provided an explanation, spoken slowly to aid my evidently deficient intellect: 'She's the size of a double bed. And she has been bed bound for the last eight years.' 'Oh, obese!' I said. 'That's what I said,' chided Mark junior, 'morbidly a beast!'

Mark junior was himself clinically obese and he couldn't keep still during the long assessment. He careered about the clinic like a caged bear. At one point, he ran out and returned with the gaudy six-foot Christmas tree from reception, its electric lights trailing forlornly. I didn't bat an eyelid. By now I had learnt to expect anything in ADHD clinic and felt that perhaps the best skill I had developed was to be able to continue to take a decent clinical history while having my hair pulled, my chair tugged or the room smashed about me by my inquisitive patients. Mark had participated in our IQ screening at various mainstream schools as part of the recruitment process for the study. It is well known that a significant proportion of children in mainstream schools have intellectual disability but are not being tested or identified, likely due to economic considerations. Mark's IQ was 62, putting him in the mild intellectual-disability range.

I saw Mark every few weeks for the next 12 weeks and he appeared no different. I hated this part of the study, as I had to put on a breezy smile of encouragement to coerce families to stay in the trial, even when I myself had begun to suspect that a child was receiving a daily dose of gravy thickener. Finally, confirmation came that Mark had been in the placebo group of the study and I hastily prescribed him the real deal. In this, the open-label part of the study, we worked on establishing an optimal dosing regime, then followed up patients at six months and one year. At six months, Mark reported to me that his teachers had given him an award for most improved behaviour. The medication side effect of appetite suppression had meant that he had lost some weight. Because of this, he was more able to participate and enjoy PE lessons. I advised that he should take this opportunity to change his diet so that he could sustain weight loss if he were to come off medication, but overall, I was glad and slightly chuffed that I had made a little difference to someone's life. At our one year follow-up, I was gobsmacked. I had to do a double-take to be sure that I was seeing the same child. Mark wore an ironed, cotton collared shirt. He'd had a haircut, was washed, clean and was a healthy weight. His freckles spread across his face as he beamed. Mark's whole attitude and self-esteem had changed; you could see it in the way he held himself. He was doing much better academically at school and he had received praise and recognition for his efforts, which encouraged him to continue. We retested his IQ and found that his test scores had improved by eight points. He had stopped misbehaving since he could actually listen to the teacher and understand what he was supposed to be doing in class. He was no longer mocked about his weight. Best of all, he had found a passion: 'I'm on the school football team,' he said. 'I didn't know I was good at it because I was always out of breath before.'

With my own eyes, during that trial, I saw the benefit of ADHD medication for a whole host of children with intellectual disability. One boy's IQ score jumped a staggering 15 points, moving him out of the intellectual-disability range altogether. But I don't want to give the false impression that it suits everybody equally. For some children like Mark, the effects were life-changing, while for others, they were more marginal. A handful of the 120 patients dropped out of the trial because of side effects. Most of these had an additional ASD diagnosis and it was later shown in the sub-analysis that children with ASD are more susceptible to adverse medication side effects. Overall though, the study was able to show that methylphenidate was significantly beneficial in the treatment of ADHD in children with intellectual disability beyond the benefits of placebo, and the vast majority of families decided to continue medication for their children after the trial ended, which perhaps speaks for itself.

Becoming a paediatric neuropsychiatrist

I had thought I had it all figured out in terms of finding my own sense of belonging. But towards the end of my time on the ADHD trial, I remember a discussion between myself and my supervisor about lifestyle choices. She mentioned how specialising in paediatric neuropsychiatry had been a salva-tion for her, that it fit in much better with having a family than specialising in adolescent depression, where the risks of suicide, self-harm and subsequent clinician stress and anxiety were high, and the responsibility was perhaps irreconcilable with parenting. Perhaps she knew better than I did my own mental health limitations. As I had always known that I wanted to be first and foremost a mother and was still shaken by the memory of Johnny's suicide, this was advice that I was ready to consider.

To begin with, when I started in child psychiatry clinical training, it felt like going back to school. I was learning new and wonderful things, and I was surrounded by kids again. Not only those at work, but also my own. I had become a mother to Molly, a beautiful baby girl with large brown eyes, rosebud mouth and a stubbornness I recognised as my own. Becoming a parent was one of my life's ambitions, but just because I desired it, it didn't mean it was easy. Nor, as I was to discover, was working as a junior doctor in post-2008-financial-crisis-austerity Britain.

Non-conformism and loss of workplace belonging

Having taken several years out for research and maternity leave, I returned to clinical training in my seventh year as a junior doctor. It wasn't just that the shift rotas had become unfairly inflexible with only month-on-month release (particularly impossible for people who had to arrange childcare to cover on-call commitments).* I was also perturbed to find after my maternity leave that I had been reassigned as a new starter, with my pay therefore downgraded.** With nursery bills and a mortgage to pay, I flagged this to management, expecting that the mistake would be corrected. But the heyday of those early junior doctor days when we were treated like talented trainees to be taught and nurtured were over. Fragile from sleep deprivation, overstretched from full-time work and full-on parenting, fraught with financial worry, I ugly-cried

---

* With month-on-month rota release, doctors can be made to cover their colleagues' maternity or long-term sick leave without realising it, thereby relieving trusts of their responsibility to employ locums.

** There are legal frameworks that prevent downgrading of pay for employees who go on maternity leave, and pay-protection clauses in doctors' contracts so that mortgages can be obtained and honoured.

in the office. Eventually, I sought advice from my union, the British Medical Association (BMA). Within days, the illegal rota system was removed and my on-call pay was restored, as it is illegal to penalise staff for taking maternity leave. However, my 'assertiveness' had been noted by management; I was branded as trouble, having declined to 'take one for the team'. At the time, I was too busy to let it bother me and just carried on.

A year later, I gave birth to my son, D (this is what we always called him as it means little brother in Chinese), a chubby, cheery fellow with a full head of hair. The impact of a second child cannot be underestimated. Having more than one child under the age of five years to look after is hard work. Indeed, having three or more children under the age of five years is a recognised risk factor for clinical depression. For me, the financial, emotional and physical burden of parenting while also working full-time as a doctor was immense. Something had to give. On my return to work after my second round of maternity leave, I had only six months left of specialist training before I could start applying for consultant posts. I therefore made the decision to complete my training full-time with two infants; but I vowed to myself and my children that once qualified, I would only look for part-time consultant work.

Depressingly, when I returned to work, I was again rebranded as a new starter and had my pay docked. In disbelief, I contacted HR and explained that they had made a mistake, I was returning from maternity leave and was not a new starter and that reducing my pay was illegal. Again, I was rebuffed as the 'mistaken' one. Realising that this time the salary they had assigned me would not even cover my childcare – I would be paying to go to work – I didn't hesitate to call the BMA. My pay was restored the next day. Farcical is not too strong a description. It was this hardening position from management, driven top down by government austerity measures, that later culminated in a harsh new contract for junior doctors, leading to unprecedented strikes in 2016. The betrayal that junior doctors felt from an organisation they thought they had belonged to was immense and resulted in the haemorrhaging of clinical goodwill and the departure of many good doctors from the NHS.

By now, although I had had ambitions to work at a teaching hospital, to continue to teach and participate in research, I knew that my days of data analysis and journal publications were over. Research requires dedication and many late nights spent bent over a computer. My late nights were now spent pat-patting children to sleep, singing the theme tune of *Neighbours* as a passable lullaby. I spent my last months as a trainee frantically treading water with the feeling that I might drown at any moment. A decade ago or so, part-time consultant work in London was scarce, and I failed my first consultant interview. The feedback from the interview panel was that I was 'too hesitant', which was not a virtue given that consultant roles required leadership. Figuring that for me at that point any part-time consultant post would suffice, I gladly accepted a non-teaching-hospital consultant job in Hertfordshire.

Positive reframe

Lives can be transformed not just by large changes in action but also by small changes in perspective and interpretation. For example, it is through political rhetoric and a media lens that we absorb news and events and form opinions. According to newspapers, junior doctors were 'rude, arrogant and lazy' circa 2016 but in

2020 these same people became 'Covid heroes' 'putting their lives at risk to help fight the spread of the coronavirus'.[27] Junior doctors have always been the same people getting on with their jobs; it is how society wishes to perceive and portray them that has apparently changed. In the same way, although we are all born with different abilities, it is parents, families, schools, communities and society that dictate whether these abilities are seen as good or bad, beautiful or ugly, strengths or weaknesses. It is society's choice, for example, not to provide enough support for kids with ADHD, instead branding them as 'naughty'; or not to provide enough ramps for people in wheelchairs, thus exacerbating disability; or not to give support to adults with special needs, labelling them 'unemployable' instead. Too often people are viewed in discrete groups, of 'sane' and 'insane', 'men' and 'women', or 'black' and 'white', and 'us' and 'them' instead of 'we'. Who 'belongs' and who 'doesn't belong' are merely points of view, which are infinitely corrodible and changeable, depending on how a society looks at itself at any particular time. This is not rocket science but it is a point that still clearly needs to be made: as human beings, we are all part of this society that can support or reject others; and we all have the choice to be tolerant and accepting or hostile and unsupportive.

For the most part, changing our attitude doesn't even come at much tangible cost; it just requires a different perspective. With the coining of terms such as neurodiversity and gender identity, and public calls for respect and equal opportunity for people of all diversities, the future is looking more positive.

6

Sh*t happens: the impact of adverse life events and trauma

One of the fundamental benefits of belonging is the security it gives. When we belong, we feel safe and in control of our environment. We know what's what, who to trust and what to expect. So it is particularly damaging when unexpected sh*t happens and rocks our sense of where we belong and robs us of this safety. For example, children's lives can be turned upside down when their parents separate or divorce, an event that is fundamentally out of their control.

Similarly, no matter what we do or how much we pray, cancer and dementia can progress despite treatment, and loved ones will be stolen from us. For many of us, experiencing a loss of control – whether it be due to a collapse in a relationship, or health, or finances – can bring on feelings of anxiety and hopelessness. When we lose control of our life, it is worse than losing our place of belonging; it is about losing ourselves. Life becomes about survival, and recovery from such a systemic breakdown is slow. It involves having to come to terms with our life experiences, perhaps accepting a changed identity and establishing a new reality that we can live with.

Leona was a girl whose life had fallen apart following a

severely traumatic incident in adolescence. When I first met her during training on the adolescent unit, the décor immediately told me that this was to be the polar-opposite ward environment to Mental Health of the Elderly. Instead of chintz and plaid winged armchairs, there were bright-yellow beanbags, and instead of Vera Lynn there was Linkin Park (this was 2010); the whole ward was clean lines and bright pops of colour.

And yet… here as with my previous experience of working with the elderly, there was a strong unifying factor in the patients' distress: the lack of a sense of belonging. In this case, all the patients on the ward were grappling with adolescent hormonal changes and searching for identity. For most of them, this was their first brush with severe mental health problems.

The statistics in child and adolescent mental health make for grim reading. Research has shown that 75% of adult mental health problems will have started before people even reach their early twenties; 50% will have had symptoms prior to the age of 14.[28]

The 2017 Mental Health of Young People survey showed that an astounding 1 in 8 children aged 5–19 years have a mental health condition, the most at-risk age group being those in late adolescence (17–19 years). In this group, 17% (that's 1 in 6 teenagers) have a mental health condition (mainly emotional problems), and approximately half of them self-harm or attempt suicide, and 1 in 20 (that's approximately one teenager in every A-level class) is already taking some form of psychotropic medication (mainly anti-depressants).[29]

The impact of catastrophe: Leona's story

Leona's story is best told as she wrote it herself:

Leona waved goodbye to her parents for the Easter holidays. They were going back to Nigeria to attend her cousin Priscilla's wedding. They would stay a few weeks extra as the airfare was so expensive that they wanted to make sure that they saw all the family, especially Grandma, who didn't have long left to live. Leona had helped her mother to pack her new brightly coloured iro and buba, which had been especially bought for the occasion. How glorious her mother had looked in it when she tried it on the night before. Leona wished that the timing of the wedding had been better, but she had her GCSEs beginning soon and there was no question that she could have gone with her parents and wasted valuable revision time. Her mother had valiantly offered to stay with her, but Leona had insisted that she go. She was 16 now, she'd be fine for two weeks by herself in London. She'd just be studying; peace and quiet in the home would actually suit her. Her father made arrangements for his younger brother, Uncle Derek, to pop by now and again to check that she was OK.

Leona had thought staying home alone would be a breeze, but by day four, it had started to become boring and eerily quiet. She became grateful for the hustle-and-bustle sounds of next door and even her two-year-old neighbour's screaming tantrums were a welcome break from her geography revision. Was it necessary to know about relief rainfall when you were going to be the next Vivienne Westwood? She began to let her routine slip and before long she was struggling to stay awake; she'd take a nap on the settee, only to wake at 6 or 7pm in a state of panic over the wasted day,

*working late into the night instead. Tinned chicken soup
was her primary companion, but on Saturday, she'd budg-
eted for a trip to the Pizza Hut on the high street. Divine.*

*But there was to be no Pizza Hut on Saturday. As usual,
she had fallen asleep on the sofa, only to be jolted awake by
a hand over her mouth and a pushing at her groin. She
wasn't sure if she was awake or dreaming at first, but the
pain was all too real. She gasped for air as the hand pushed
down, stifling any sound she might make – although she
didn't even try as she was desperately trying to find air to
take in, in order to stay alive. The room was shrouded in
the semi-darkness of twilight, but Leona discerned the face
of Uncle Derek bearing down on her, his stale, intoxicated
breath on her cheek and his body pressed hard against her
entire torso, making it impossible for her to move. To her
horror her knickers were at her ankles, and the meaning of
the ripping pain at her groin became all too apparent. At the
point where she realised what was happening and considered
fighting back as an option, it was all over. She was released,
a soiled rag discarded on the settee. She didn't dare move.
She heard him flushing the toilet. A shadow hesitated at the
doorway for a split second – was there something to be said?
– and then fled.*

*Leona did not know what to do. She lay there for an
indeterminate time. She did not know whether she could
move, but as the hours rolled on and the air turned chilly,
she knew that she would have to try. Her whole being ached
as she tried to process what had happened. Perhaps it had
been a dream. The house was quiet once more. There was
her desk, there were her study guides, there was her revision
timetable; neatly copied out and taped to the wall. There
was her folder of badass dress designs, just as she had left
them. A bad, bad dream.*

The shrill of the phone broke her from her daze. It was her mother, all excitement after Priscilla's wedding. Priscilla's dress was fabulous, her husband lucky, the ceremony long. Aunty Rejoice had put on considerable weight. Papa did too much dancing, imagined he was ten years younger and was now suffering the consequences. Little Adebayo was now big Adebayo, complete with facial hair, and baby Imo was the cutest thing, although her mother was still too thin to be attractive. 'And we hear that you had a nice time with Uncle Derek. He took you to Pizza Hut and you had a double portion of Meat Feast. Lucky you! How he has always spoilt you.' Leona's mouth could not open. Her brain was having difficulty computing what was happening. What was her mother saying about Uncle Derek? What could she say now about the matter? Her entire being was numb. She wanted nothing more than to cleanse herself, over and over and over. In the shower later, she scrubbed at her body repeatedly, but it was her mind that she could not cleanse.

The next morning, she tried to pretend that nothing had happened. There was her study desk. There were her books. She sat at her desk, but nothing was going in. She stared vacantly into space. Time passed inordinately quickly. Day merged into night and back into day. There would be no sleeping on the settee today. There would never be sleeping on the settee ever again. She drew the curtains, triple locked the doors and windows and moved a large chair to block the front door.

When Leona's parents returned, they were laden with gifts and photos. 'You've been terribly quiet?' voiced her mother, and 'Why have you got so thin? The amount of times Uncle Derek has taken you out to eat, I'd have thought you'd be twice the weight by now! Which reminds me, I need to pay him back because he can't be treating you so often. Papa, call him now and invite him over for supper, that's the least we can do.'

It was then that Leona finally found her voice, with an instinctive outpouring of the bottled pain of the last few weeks. Her parents did not know what had come over her. Leona shook uncontrollably, she gagged at the imagery of Uncle Derek's face, she tried to push it out of her mind, but it kept returning, each time more vivid and twisted. She could not see him again.

Her mother was quick to accept Leona's account of events, but it took time for her father. Derek was his brother, someone he had raised since boyhood when their mother had worked long hours at the hospital. Then had come the anger; it took all of her mother's strength to barricade the door to prevent her father leaving to vent his rage on his brother. Then had come the guilt. Why had he not been there to protect his precious daughter?

Would Leona be responsible for the imprisonment of a previously beloved uncle? Was Leona strong enough to be able to press charges against him? These were not questions Leona wanted to think about. She didn't want to think about anything. Leona wanted the world to rewind, or failing that, for the ground to open up and swallow her whole. In the day, numbness was her sanctuary. If she stayed very still, she could survive the day without the smell of her predator's breath invading her senses, but by night, she had little control, and often her mother would have to run in and hold her. It was then that she realised that she had not once cried since the incident.

After the holidays, Leona found it impossible to return to school. She could no longer relate to her girlfriends' chatter about GCSEs and plans for the parties after them. She did not want to look at her crush Marcus, even though she had spent most of the year trying to get him to look at her. Although the teachers had to be told, Leona did not want her friends to know what had happened to her. The shame would be too much. She was different now; tarnished. She was out of step and did not belong. Months later, GCSEs postponed, her mother decided to take her to see a child psychiatrist. The child psychiatrist pitied her, she could tell that by her sad face and quiet tone. She wanted to scream, 'Don't pity me! I am Leona. I am a Lion. I am the next Vivienne Westwood!' but she couldn't, she could barely whisper. She wondered if she was permanently broken.

One day Leona got out a pen and paper. The child psychiatrist had told her about post-traumatic stress disorder and how her symptoms fitted with this. That although it felt like numbness was all she could experience now, she was strong, she was a lion, like her name. Her mother had shown the child psychiatrist her folder of fashion designs, so that she could understand who Leona was before. The child psychiatrist told her to write her story down. That it was impossible to shut out hurt – the hurt needed to be let out, experienced and processed in order to dissipate. That, as in the case of a weakened dam, it was better to let the water out to cause controlled damage and open the way for the possibility of rebuilding, rather than live life in constant fear of a violent bursting. 'Focus on writing exact facts and details of what happened to you, how you felt at each moment, the sounds, the smells, the thoughts. We will work on writing and rewriting your story, over and over again, until the facts, smells and sounds are so well known to you that they cannot bother you any more. Write about it in the third person so that you can view things objectively. We will work on the narrative of your story, so that you are in control of it. We will get you through this and help you rebuild your life; but *first, we need you to be brave and face it, actively relive the events in your mind, and put it down on paper.'*

Leona took up her pen and the words eventually came, 'Leona waved goodbye to her parents for the Easter holidays' and as she wrote, she noticed that the letters were smudged. The rainfall had finally arrived, and it was a relief.

Leona's trauma was sudden, severe and life-threatening. Post-traumatic stress disorder is common after such events, with many patients describing a feeling of dissociation from themselves and the people around them. This feeling of disconnection, vacancy and numbness, of being untethered with no secure ground under our feet, is the feeling of no longer belonging to our bodies, to ourselves.

The slow erosion of mental health

In the same way that gradual erosion can cause as much devastation to a landscape as a sudden landslide, the accumulation of adverse life experiences can wreak as much destruction as a severe, one-off life event. We eventually reach a tipping point and everything falls apart. It was early on in my psychiatric training, when I was working on a general adult ward, that I realised the full impact of this, through the story of a man named Femo.

Femo was a young man of Nigerian heritage who was admitted to hospital with emerging paranoia and psychosis. He was brought to hospital by his mother, with whom he lived and who had become increasingly concerned about his strange behaviour. Femo had come to the UK to join his mother at the age of 13 years. His mother had left him in Nigeria as a child so that she could go to work as a nurse in the NHS, and he was brought up by his grandmother in their home village. He had always known that the plan was for him to join his mother someday when he was older, when she had managed to secure a home in London for them, and he was promised a better education. He had looked forward to going to London, such an exciting place and the home of his favourite football team. His mother had been sending money regularly to his grandmother and she had described a comfortable home, a well-paid job and welcoming neighbours. Her stories of the wonderful community in London had brought immense comfort to him as he had lain tearful in his bed as a child. He was missing his mother, and he knew that she missed him too, but at least she sounded happy. She always told him that their current sorrow would be superseded by the wonderful life that they would have together in London soon.

Only, when he arrived in South London at the age of 13, he found things were not quite how his mother had described. His mother looked thin and drawn. It dawned on Femo that she had sent him the majority of her wages and saved for their weekly phone call the majority of her sunshine. In reality, the sky and buildings here were drained of colour; just like his mother. The wind and rain chilled him to the bone, and his mother's flat was a concrete bedsit, sandwiched between rows of other concrete bedsits. The lift, when it was working, smelt of piss and the children next door spat at him. He would have preferred to have been back in his village. At least the chickens didn't spit. The education he was promised consisted of copying text he didn't understand from battered books defaced by crude drawings and routine beatings in the play-ground. These playground beatings were at least with fists and feet, and did not involve the sheer life-threatening fear he later faced when he inadvertently stumbled across some kids in a park where he shouldn't have been. He never ran faster in his life, disappearing into the ether like everyone else as the echo of a police siren sounded.

After leaving school, without the qualifications he had hoped for, Femo started to work with his uncle, doing small odd jobs, such as painting, decorating, home removals and taking junk to the tip in a little white van. The work was easy for a fit, strong, young man like Femo. His uncle, on the other hand, became progressively shorter of breath with time and Femo found that more and more, he had to carry the workload. Before long, although he was only 50 years old, his uncle had to call it a day, on account of recurrent bronchitis and a back injury sustained from a lifetime of heavy lifting. In return for a cut of his takings, he handed over to Femo, aged 23 years, the keys of his white van, the central asset of the business.

Perhaps it was his youthful looks and big build that made him stand out, but as soon as he was sat alone behind the wheel of the vehicle, Femo began to get noticed by the police. After the first two stop-and-searches, he figured that he should avoid wearing sunglasses even in the heat of summer, because perhaps that was what was causing offence. The first thing the police always did was ask him to take them off. He had been so scared the first time he was stopped. The policemen had spoken to him like some of the teachers had done when he was back at school, as if he were hard of hearing. He complied with everything that he was asked to do, fearful after the stories that he had heard of other people in the neighbourhood who had ended up in police cells for not doing as they were told. Guilt announced itself from nowhere; perhaps he had done something wrong. Perhaps his 70-year-old client Mr Owusu was a drug dealer and his battered old fridge that was destined for the tip was hiding a stash and he was the ignorant courier. The sniffer dog seemed to think so, the way it was nosing around. After the next two stop-and-searches, Femo stopped playing music on his radio, because this too seemed to cause offence. He began to wonder what the police were looking for, as every time he was stopped, they would rummage through the back of his van, intent on finding something. One time, old lady Derby's dresser got broken by the policeman's rummaging and she took it out of his pay. She didn't have time for his explanations of the whys and wherefores. Femo started to get angry; he needed to help his mother with the rent. Her type 2 diabetes wasn't getting any better.

He started to document the dates and times of the stop-and-searches in a little book that he kept in his glove compartment. He began to see a pattern to things. Tuesday at 10:33 am, Friday at 4:24pm, then Monday at 11:45am. You see: the number of the minutes always ended in a multiple of three. He began his own predictions about when he was going to be stopped and searched and, at these times, he would be vigilant of the cars around him. One of them was bound to be a cop car in disguise. On one occasion, the same red Jetta tailed him from Old Kent Road all the way to Elephant and Castle. He was able to shake their tail at the big roundabout somewhere between the open market and the Tabernacle.

The flat Femo shared with his mother was the only refuge from the police. But his mother worked the night shift so often that it seemed they only passed each other like ships in the night. He noticed she was getting older, her bifocals resting on top of her grey hair as she sank into the armchair in the mornings after a shift and massaged her aching arches as he handed her a cup of tea. A lifetime of three sugars, perhaps the root of her diabetes, was her only vice. Carelessly, she opened the brown envelope that sat on the coffee table and drew her bifocals down onto her nose. She let out a groan. 'Femo!' she said. 'You've been caught on them speeding cameras down by the Tabernacle.'

This confirmed to Femo that his whereabouts were being monitored by the police. Not only were they able to attack him on the streets, they now had CCTV cameras everywhere that were watching him. He couldn't sit around any longer letting them target him in this way. He had to act.

He returned from the store late, just as his mother was leaving for work. 'There's a roast for you in the oven, Femo. I know you do like your roasts,' she chuckled, rubbing his cheek gently. 'You look tired. You must get to bed early.' But he had no intention of sleeping; he had work to do. He emptied out the plastic bag of supplies he had bought from the hardware store: heavy-duty tin foil and gaffer tape.

When his mother returned from her shift the next morning, Femo was finally asleep. The flat was eerily dark and she struggled to get the door open. When she stepped inside it was pitch black. The windows had been covered up by something that completely blocked out the morning light. She flicked a light switch on and it was as if her retina had been set alight. Light bounced about the room in all directions. The entire flat had been covered in baking foil, and there lay Femo in the armchair, exhausted from his labour.

The link between immigration and psychosis has been extremely well documented and identified in different populations, from African-Caribbeans in the UK to Norwegians in the United States. Work conducted by Professor Sir Robin Murray in the 1990s was key to much of this research and formed the basis of one of the current theories of schizophrenia.[30] Before meeting Femo, I'd heard the professor speak many times on this subject. He was a great storyteller, and his best story related to his attempt to test whether the high incidence rates of psychosis in the UK African-Caribbean population were related to prejudicial diagnosing. He had identified that the rates of psychosis in the UK African-Caribbean population were much higher than in the indigenous UK population, but also much higher than the rates in Jamaica and other Caribbean islands. Was there something about displacement and the immigration experience that was causing psychosis, or were the findings reflective of prejudicial diagnosing on the part of British psychiatrists (due to institutional racism, perhaps)?

Professor Murray told us how he'd sought to disentangle this question by inviting a Jamaican psychiatrist colleague to come over to the UK to assess his patients independently and see whether or not he would agree with his diagnosing. Could there be any more ironic twist in the tale? Well, yes. No sooner had the Jamaican psychiatrist arrived in the vicinity of the hospital than he was arrested by the police. Professor Murray had hired the Jamaican doctor a Mercedes Benz to drive. The sight of a black man driving a Merc around Brixton was enough to warrant arrest. His protests of 'But I'm a prominent Jamaican psychiatrist come to assist British doctors in important research on institutional racism in the UK!' unfortunately didn't do him any favours. 'Of course you are, sir!' said the police, after impounding his vehicle and taking him into custody. On his release, he was eventually able to complete his project with Professor Murray. They found that Jamaican and UK diagnosing were almost entirely comparable, confirming immigration, persecution and racial discrimination as contributory factors in psychosis, alongside genetics and biological causes.

Although it was positive that Jamaican and British psychiatrists had comparable diagnosing practices, this does not deny the existence of institutional racism in mental health. The AESOP study, conducted in 2010 by British psychiatrists and involving more than 500 patients with a serious mental health disorder from various ethnic groups, found that, 'In the UK, research has consistently shown that African-Caribbeans are not only at greater risk of developing psychosis, but are also more likely to access mental healthcare via adversarial routes, often involving the police and compulsory admission, and more likely to be treated in secure and forensic settings.'[31] These findings are certainly a cause for concern, and institutional racism continues to be a consideration. Indeed, the differences in your experience of mental healthcare depending on whether you are black British or white British start much earlier in the system. Journalist Keith Cooper summarised the findings reported in Professor Sir Simon Wessely's Independent Review of the Mental Health Act 2018 in these stark terms: 'If you are of black African or Caribbean background… you are treated differently from childhood. The research shows that for bad behaviour, you get the social worker, not the child psychologist, and are more likely to be expelled. As an adult, you have less chance of accessing talking therapies. If you do, you will face someone with whom you have little in common.'[32]

Abuse, whether it is severe, brutal and physical, and inflicted by an individual, or slow, gradual and insidiously inflicted by society, often gives rise to a feeling of alienation and lack of belonging. It leaves us feeling dirty, shameful, guilty and humiliated, and can confirm our nagging beliefs that we are flawed, unlovable and 'not good enough'. If internally we feel monstrous and inhuman, how can we feel we will ever belong?

Patients on the edge

Stories of alienation from patients like Femo are uncomfortable to read, which may explain why they are rarely heard despite being far from rare. I feel that telling their stories is important because we need to think about and act on our discomfort rather than avoid it. In my time in psychiatry training, I came across so many desperate people on the edge. There was Lauren, a 20-year-old found walking along the railway tracks at Clapham Junction naked, whom I was forced to section as her intent, were she to be permitted to leave A&E, was to do the same thing again. There was Matt, a drug addict who it took a potentially lethal dose of benzodiazepines to pacify. Matt was trying to shake off the five members of the emergency team who were struggling to hold him down. My hands shook as I inserted a cannula into the back of his hand while he repeatedly screamed, '*Get away from me, you witch doctor*', all the time writhing and shouting death threats. As he was tolerant to the medication, he needed higher doses for it to have any effect. Finally, after a dose that would have been lethal to most people, the nurses, exhausted from having held him for so long, were able to escort him to a bed. They watched over him overnight to check that he was alright and thankfully, by morning, drug-induced psychosis over, he was calm and collected once more.

Psychiatrists are perhaps the only doctors who are required to take regular courses in self-defence and 'break-away training' as part of their mandatory training. We learn how to get someone to release us if they have their hands around our neck, along with other last-resort strategies that we hope we never have to use because we are also trained in de-escalation: how to avoid situations getting out of hand in the first place, how to notice a brewing situation and to take the heat out of it. We are taught how the tone of our voice, our facial expressions and our every movement can be the difference between walking out of a room alive or being carried out on a stretcher. Yet, even with all this training, we never think it will happen to us – until the moment that we realise that it's happening.

Denise towered over me as I sat looking up at her. I wasn't able to acquiesce to her wishes. She had come into hospital voluntarily, but now, in the middle of the night, she had realised that it was a bad idea and she wanted out. Unfortunately, her mental health condition was such that she was currently a potential danger to others, and she was detainable under the doctor's emergency holding powers under the Mental Health Act. Clearly this is not news that anybody is happy to hear. The curtailing of civil liberties is drastic but at times necessary. Denise had already been pacing around the room in agitation. I had clocked the location of the door to my right and the female nurse next to the exit. I stated my apologies as calmly and considerately as possible: 'I know that you want to leave and you don't like it here, but it's really late, please at least stay until morning when your own psychiatrist can see you,' I said. 'I worry that it's not safe for you to leave and I can't let you go.' 'What gives you the right?' Denise shouted as she thumped the wall above my head. I saw the nurse tense, unsure whether to approach or keep a distance. In my seated position, I suddenly felt immensely vulnerable. If I stood up, I'd have a better chance of fighting off an attack and making it to the door, but another instinct, and perhaps the de-escalation training I had undertaken, was telling me that standing would signal a 'squaring-up' to Denise and could be an 'invitation' to her aggression. I fought my survival instinct. 'I'm sorry,' I said, staying seated and calm, not moving a muscle, in anticipation of a punch. But Denise could plainly see that she was the power player now, not I. It was perhaps because of this that she finally said, 'OK. I'll stay till morning,' and retreated. As I walked back to bed, my throat was dry and I was shaking. Her own doctor, who knew her better, could decide whether to section her in the morning.

Over time, as well as desperation, I encountered hopelessness. More and more stories of women presenting to A&E following their tenth overdose; or addicts repeatedly presenting in violent crisis. Although in my enthusiastic youth, it was not my nature to consider cases 'hopeless' from the outset, towards the tail end of psychiatric training, I could not stem the sinking feeling of futility when hospital notes came out of the hospital archives three bricks thick detailing A&E assessments and subsequent failed interventions for patients. Many of them struggled with addiction and self-harm, and their problems with mental health were intertwined with their troubled childhoods, lost education and social predicaments, most of which we as doctors had very little power to affect. Often these were people caught in vicious cycles that they could not escape. The input required to 'rescue' even one such person would need significant resources from multiple different departments in addition to health: housing, education (adult education, mentorship, apprenticeship), social care (support for domestic violence and debt management, benefits, legal advice), as well as the police. With resources being reduced simultaneously in all these areas, what hope was there of any rescue? And sometimes, I confess, it was a challenge to not give up myself. What was the purpose of my assessment, if all I could realistically offer was a few pills that had already been tried, a referral to housing that would sit on a list 100 names deep and a recommendation to the patient that they refer themself to overstretched psychological intervention services?

These people are the forgotten in society, and I am taking the time to talk about them because they deserve to be talked about and thought about. They are all someone's daughter, son, sister or brother, and although it is easier for us to turn a blind eye to their existence, they exist, and the unhappiness of their existence is the result of a cumulative failing in our society. I hope that by highlighting the sharp end of things, we can bring about more acceptance and help from society – from every one of us.

Losing myself: loss of identity in motherhood

I don't think that it is possible to remain unaffected at some level by experiences such as these, and it is acknowledged that physicians, by virtue of their uniquely stressful jobs, are highly prone to burn-out. Even after I chose to specialise in child psychiatry, on-call work could involve an 11-year-old having their stomach pumped with charcoal for an overdose or a 17-year-old who'd set his girlfriend on fire – literally. These occupational stresses are of course layered onto the everyday pressures of modern life; and for me, as for so many other working parents, it was becoming a struggle to keep all the balls in the air.

Up until the moment of childbirth, I had enjoyed financial independence. I was quite satisfied with my identity as a doctor with intelligent colleagues and friends, a healthy salary and a 50:50 domestic-chore and power dynamic with my husband. And then, unexpectedly, an unspoken change occurred on passing a melon-sized being from out of my nether regions. There had been a fundamental shift in the relationship I had with my husband, with society, with myself. It was as if my identity had been stripped away, and with it the security of my place of belonging.

Suddenly, I was no longer me. I was Mrs Andrew, or mother of my children. I was still a doctor, of course, and yet not the high-flying, ass-kicking, clinical-academic-jet -setting-to-international-conferences doctor I had set out to be. I was now the dishevelled late-for-work doctor, the OMG-I-need-you-to-cover-my-afternoon-clinic-because-my-kid's-spiked-a-temperature-and-the-nursery-won't-just-give-her-calpol-like-I-told-them-to doctor, the crying-in-the-toilets-because-sometimes-it's-too-much doctor. It was a difficult adjustment.

Outside of work, somehow the bulk of the cooking, cleaning and laundry had transitioned to being my responsibility. It had shifted there during maternity leave when I was the stay-at-home parent, and somehow never quite shifted back on my return to full-time work. Conversations with friends about politics, books and art were replaced with discussions about faecal consistency and raucous renditions of 'Jelly on a plate'. Polite small talk was replaced with 'tellings-off' (breast-feeding is not allowed here), rebukes (your baby is not wearing socks), unrequested nuggets of parenting advice (you should try turmeric), raised eyebrows (how dare she bring a baby here) and generally being spoken to like an idiot. It was as if I'd become someone else entirely. Like anyone who struggles with retirement, maternity for me was like a mini identity crisis. I didn't belong with the athleisure-wear mums, but I also no longer belonged with my academic psychiatry chums.

Although I was able to continue with my career as a psychiatrist, it was not a career at the level that I had been used to. In the smaller, quieter hospital in Hertfordshire, while I had excellent and committed colleagues, some of whom also became good friends, I missed that feeling of being at the 'cutting edge' of science. And so, after a few years, as Molly and D were soon to be both of school age and I no longer had to contend with steep childcare costs, I made the decision that I could afford to take a part-time fellowship post at trainee pay (despite having been a consultant for three years), in order to return to the bright lights and ivory towers of the big city university hospital.

I was welcomed back with open arms by old colleagues and friendly faces. It felt like coming home. Almost immediately, I was asked by a previous supervisor, Professor Carmichael, a trailblazing female academic at the top of her game, to apply for a full-time consultant post to lead a national service with her. But the timing was all wrong; my children were still so young. When I declined to apply, as I was insistent on part-time working, I was told that I would never be able to work part-time in a prestigious teaching hospital. Didn't I realise that I couldn't have it all? I should focus on my career and hire a nanny as she had done. I have absolutely no doubt that her words were meant in kindness: a blueprint for 'how to become a successful female in a male-dominated world'. She had shared with me on occasion the tough calls that she herself had had to make and the personal sacrifices. Had I been childless at the time, had I been the family breadwinner, had my husband had a more flexible job, had society endorsed women to go all out on their careers, or had I been a man, I'd have leapt at it. Professor Carmichael must have thought me crazy and ungrateful, but she had me all wrong. I entered child psychiatry because I am all about the children, and now mine came first.

Meanwhile life went on. Andrew called me from his work trip in Singapore, his twelfth work trip abroad that year – I had been coping single-handed in his absence. 'I'm shattered,' he said, 'the flight was delayed and now I'm in a taxi stuck in traffic.' Perhaps he was expecting sympathy, but his day sounded like bliss – reading, movie watching and sleeping in business class without the wailing of two toddlers. 'I'm really sorry, I can't talk right now,' I said, 'D has thrown up all over the back seat of the car so I'm cleaning up his puke with a bucket and sponge. I've had to cancel work, because obviously nursery won't take him now.'

My daughter broke her leg, my father was diagnosed with early myeloma (blood cancer), my sister had a breast lump investigated. For all purposes, because I was a doctor, I was the chief hospital escort. 'I'm really sorry, I'm going to need to take that day off work – I'll make the time up.' Thank goodness I was working part-time so I could. People needed me. I gritted my teeth and carried on. I reassured my sister that at her age a lump was likely benign. It wasn't. I accompanied her to the scan of her other one. I reassured her that we had caught it early; it couldn't have spread to the other breast. It had. I couldn't reassure her any more and she had a double mastectomy. I visited her in hospital after the surgery and brought her macaroons, but ate them all myself as she wasn't hungry.

The one advantage of austerity from my point of view was that, as the NHS tried to make savings by reducing consultant sessions where possible, contrary to what Prof Carmichael had told me, more and more part-time consultant posts started being advertised in child psychiatry. Eventually, even competitive teaching hospitals started to advertise part-time posts. As my research fellowship came to a close, I applied for a locum position at a familiar trust, but I failed to get it, losing out to a white female trainee with no consultant experience. I knew my CV and references were good as I had reduced waiting times in my service in Hertfordshire from over a year to under three months, so was at a loss as to what could have gone so wrong for me at interview. Asking for feedback from a consultant after my interview failure, he told me: 'Reputation here is really important and you have a reputation for being forthright and assertive.' I wondered how I could have gone from 'hesitant' to 'assertive' in an interview situation within a matter of a few years and how both were considered objectionable. I wondered whether he was hinting at my former 'assertiveness' as a trainee where I had stood up to managers for my legal pay rights. The brazen audacity!

For men, being forthright and assertive is often taken as a marker of ambition and a virtue for leadership, and I was shocked to hear this consultant explicitly clarify his position that assertiveness in women was undesirable, while throwing in a bit of casual racism for good measure: 'We British don't like it.' It finally clicked: despite having lived in Britain for nearly 40 years and held a British passport for the majority of that time, regardless of my Cambridge medical degree, my received pronunciation, my western outlook on life and normcore dressing, I was not seen as 'British'. I might as well have been wearing a chi pao and serving oolong tea. In a single conversation, my identity as a good doctor, a valued NHS employee and a British citizen had been stripped from me. Worse still, despite being apparently so 'forthright and assertive', I found I could think of no comeback. Humiliation had silenced me, and I realised that not only had I lost myself, I'd also lost my voice.

Physician on the ledge

I felt physically sick but still had to pick up the children and go through the motions of dinner, bath time and story time. An argument ensued later with Andrew: 'You're really good at your job, something will come up'; his words, meant to comfort, grated severely; years of pent-up tension and bitterness were unleashed: 'Do you understand that I turned down applying for my dream job, for the family?'; and 'Do you know what it feels like when someone says, 'We British don't like it'?' It feels like: 'Go back to where you came from, you are not one of us and never will be – we British don't like you.' I went to bed early with a headache and tossed and turned all night, contemplating all the things in my life that seemed to be spinning away from me.

I ruminated about the insane challenges of parenthood. There was no time alone to think. Who would have thought that going to the toilet alone would become a privilege? The relentless chores, the routines and the day-to-day responsibilities. Anything the children did/didn't do/ate/didn't eat; any harm/potential harm/possibility of harm that might have befallen them, it was down to me. I thought about the tension in my relationship with Andrew. We'd been together since we were 21. We'd lasted the long-distance part and were finally married with a family, but now I felt like he was on another planet. He was continuing the same working hours we both used to work, wining and dining clients late at night, and saying things like 'Why should both careers suffer?' and 'We talked about this, you were the one that didn't want to hire a nanny'. All I could think was: why does he get to carry on as if nothing has happened? Why doesn't he understand? Maybe he doesn't love me any more… how could he love me with my tracksuit pants and stretch marks when there were younger women at his work who still wore high heels and make-up and didn't have ham in their hair? Why else would he work long hours and not come home? Had he ever loved me? I've let myself go. I didn't feel wholly supported or understood by my husband and therefore pushed him away. I felt alone in our relationship.

I thought about the stress of my work; about the upkeep of a gruelling workload squeezed into a shorter day, lest colleagues and superiors should arch an eyebrow or make a comment insinuating that I was not 'pulling my weight'; the absorption of the angry, helpless, desperate stories of hundreds of people, day in, day out. The anxiety, second-guessing and fear over whether my decision-making was correct as the catastrophic consequences of wrong decisions played out in my mind. There was also the immense anxiety that I was next in the redundancy line. Unemployment had never even been on my radar. I was great at my job. Or was I? Each rejection tilted the balance in my mind towards my own resounding self-doubt. Maybe I wasn't so good after all. Look at the people that I had tried to help. I was pretty certain that on discharge from the eating disorders unit, Sophie would have relapsed into anorexia – 60% of patients do following their first inpatient admission; many go on to die a premature death.[33] And Hayley: every single A&E shift I covered, I fully expected to see teenage Hayley come in with slashed wrists. I never saw her; but I saw many just like her.

I'd made a good run of it, pretending to be competent. I'd always felt an imposter, and now I'd been found out. I deserved to be unemployed. Going forward in any case was about leadership potential, and did I really think that I had that? I wasn't management material: 'too hesitant', 'too asser-tive', 'too forthright', 'too unlikable' for British people – one of whom I was not. It suddenly became clear to me that despite my shapeshifting as a child and adult, despite my attempts to bend this way and that to gain acceptance from the people around me, ultimately, what most people saw was my gender and the colour of my skin. It suddenly became clear: it didn't matter what I did or didn't do; I'd never belong in the higher tiers of a British workplace or British society.

By early morning, I was sleep deprived and shattered, having spent the night duelling my greatest adversary: myself. I looked in the mirror and I didn't recognise what I saw. I acknowledged that for a while now I had been going through the motions of each day feeling detached and dissociated from life; firefighting to survive, doing what I needed to do just to get by. My identity at the time was heavily staked on being a hard-working British doctor – and yet now I was staring unemployment in the face. It was difficult for me at that time to see this as anything other than abject failure. Was life even worth living?

In that instant, I had the feeling that I could not breathe; in hindsight this was most likely a panic attack. I went to the window and opened it wide, leaning out far to take in as much air as I could. The morning air was delicious. The treetops of the heath that I looked down upon were beautiful in the gentle morning light. Calm and inviting. My mind was numb and before I knew it, I was on the window ledge looking down at my toes, contemplating oblivion.

Moving on from the brink

Looking back over that time in my life is difficult. Today, when I look at my CV and at my wonderful children, I think, 'Wow – did I really do all that?', because on paper, it sounds impressive. But the reality is that it came at a great cost to me. These days, whenever I hear women compare themselves to someone who looks, sounds and appears perfect and has a great many accomplishments on paper, I don't wonder like them, 'I don't know how she does it!'; I only think, 'I wonder why she does it? And at what cost to her?'

We all seem to lead increasingly busy lives. Our routines have become more and more complicated compared to those of our own parents. In the old days, men went to work and women looked after the home and children. In many ways, the increased independence of women has been our emancipation, but for some women it has meant assuming a multitude of time-consuming roles, which only add to their daily burden. Women have taken it upon themselves to be kick-ass at work, sometimes requiring them to take on the system to do so, yet somehow have not been unshackled from their domestic responsibilities of housework, childcare and care of elderly relatives (often not through the lack of trying). They continue to be judged more harshly in parenting, caring and friendships if they do not demonstrate 'feminine' qualities of kindness, empathy and compassion. During Covid, it has been women's work that has suffered most: they have been the main victims of furlough and redundancy, as well as reduced work productivity due to home-schooling.[34]

Not that it has been totally plain sailing for men. Over the past three or four decades, they have had to wrestle with an emerging new world order without the support of a blueprint or guidance on what is expected of them. They have had to work doubly hard to maintain employment, now facing stiff competition from talented women, and in the knowledge that unemployment will be heavily judged. Rather than a pipe and slippers, they return home to overstressed wives and a child-care role that no teacher, film, book or TV programme has prepared them for. They've participated in far more parenting, housework and care of ageing parents than their own fathers, yet their wives remain frustrated.

With these shaken rules of identity, it is no wonder that more and more of us feel that we are constantly on a treadmill. We have no time or can't cope; society is unfair towards us and has challenged our notions about where we belong. It is also these exact same fears and feelings that provoke us, just like an insecure child, to look for someone to scapegoat and blame. The white men blocking our promotion, femi-nazis demanding employment quotas, the husband who doesn't pull his weight or the nagging wife, the immigrants next door, the poor who freeload benefits and the rich who avoid paying taxes... Blaming someone else enables us to protect ourselves – although alienating others to make ourselves feel better only works for so long.

In the meantime, we follow our instinct that we must simply grin and bear it: keeping calm and carrying on is hardwired into us. In Chinese, there are also maxims about 'swallowing pain' and 'tolerating suffering' as if these were the virtues of a perfect society. But these stoical adages are outdated and maladapted to an age of increased mental health awareness. The slogan 'keep calm and carry on' was a PR exercise to manage wartime panic. Its purpose was to protect the country, not individual mental health, and they are not words to live by in peace time. Likewise, the stereotypical British 'stiff upper lip' has led to generations of damage from repressed and unprocessed emotions, seeping down through parenting to stunt the emotional growth of the next generation. Take it from a psychiatrist: in well-being terms, burying emotions is not to be recommended.

One of the most important ways we can start addressing our mental health is by making time for ourselves. Sometimes we need to step back from our lives and view them objectively in order to begin the hard work of healing. So many of us, myself included, wait till a crisis point before we are able to see that change is needed. From starting the day on the brink of the window ledge, with the mild morning sun on my face, I ended up looking at furniture in an architectural salvage yard with my husband. Andrew had found me on the windowsill. After he took the children to school, we both took the day off work and we drove out to Oxford... just because. Looking back at my own experiences, my healing started on that day.

Although we did nothing of significance, something of

great significance had happened. My husband and I both took a day off work to be together, without being physically sick. This had never happened before as both of us were ambitious and career driven – we usually went to work even when ill – so this signified something vital to me. We were finally taking time for ourselves. It was an undisclosed statement that my mental health was important to me and to him. It was a break from the hamster wheel – a chance to think about life and where we were both going and whether we were going together.

From that point on, I recognised the importance of 'me-time'. A moment that gives us space to rest and reflect, and for the mind to have time to recover; a mental sit-down in life's marathon.

Make time to relax

In our busy lives, engaging in activities for pure pleasure (for example cycling, a book club, sewing circle, art class or choir) tends to be marginalised in favour of doing activities 'with a purpose'. But acknowledging that we all need enjoyment and pleasure in life for our own well-being is crucial.

Many hobbies – particularly those that entail regular attendance with a group – involve a 'behavioural activation' as well as a social element, both of which have been shown to be protective for mental health. Behavioural activation basically means making yourself do something because the act of doing something rather than nothing makes you feel better.[35] Learning, making and achieving things is satisfying in and of itself and gaining competence empowers us. Knowing that other people are relying on us to attend a group activity is also helpful as it encourages us to get out when we may not feel like it, and the benefit of belonging and social support is healing.

Some professionals get sucked into working excessively and head down the road towards burn-out because work has consumed their social lives to the extent that they have no time for anything except their job and possibly socialising with work colleagues. Addressing this imbalance is really important; try to sustain or grow relationships outside of work. This not only allows you social space outside of the office, but provides you with a consistent support circle should an employment terminate. For stay-at-home parents, it is equally vital to carve out time outside of home and domesticity.

Even solitary hobbies, such as pottery or gardening, are good. The mental health rewards of being creative and nurturing something cannot be underestimated. This is why so many mental health facilities encourage patients to express themselves through art and offer opportunities to do activities such as gardening or cooking.

Make time to think and introspect

While disconnecting from the stress of busy lives is helpful, if there are problems in your life with regards to work, relationships or an absence of belonging, disconnection is not a satisfactory long-term remedy. No amount of yoga or mindful colouring will bring a marriage back from the brink or help you establish a relationship with your child. Ultimately, in order to improve our lives, we need to spend time analysing and reflecting on them. Setting aside space for this is important. Some people prefer to do this with a therapist, but it is by no means a requirement. In Part Three, I outline a few opening self-help steps that you can take.

7

Shame: the ongoing stigma of poor mental health

As I have said, many people hold negative preconceptions about those with mental health problems. My husband was no different. Andrew and I had dinner plans with his friend Chris, who had flown in from Australia for a mutual friend's wedding. We were looking forward to seeing him again and catching up. I told Andrew, 'Let's not be late – meet me at the hospital at 6pm and we can go to the restaurant together.'

At 6pm, I duly met Andrew at the hospital entrance. 'Wow', he said. 'So, this is where you work!' 'Well, yes, this is the outside,' I replied. 'No, really,' he said, 'I arrived early so asked reception where I could find you. They told me the name of the ward, so I went to find you – only I didn't make it because when I came up to the ward entrance there was a big black man staring through the glass pane in the door. He was leaning on it and tapping against the glass, looking left and right. He was very agitated and his mouth was drooling and foaming. I didn't dare disturb him, so I came back out to wait here.'

He looked visibly shaken following his first experience of entering a psychiatric hospital. Just the words 'psychiatric hospital' are enough to produce a shudder down the spine in many people outside the world of mental health. For me, the ward was my office; it wasn't even locked.

'Oh yes,' I said. 'That'll be Femo. He's always waiting for his mum to bring him his roast chicken dinner on a Friday evening. I'd be anxious too if my roast was late; the hospital food is bloody awful. He's a lovely bloke, I chat with him every day. Unfortunately, the medication I'm giving him makes him oversalivate; we've been trying to find one that'll work better for him.' We laughed at Andrew's abject fear of a bloke waiting for his mother as we went to dinner, but it reminded me again of my childhood response to the boy in the cage. Most of what we fear about mental health is in our imagination, stoked by misinformation. If we take the time to understand people and their circumstances, there is often nothing to fear at all.

The stigma of mental health fuels a reluctance in some people to seek psychiatric assessment and diagnosis, which can do them considerable harm. As a psychiatrist, I am open and accepting of all mental health conditions and I wish more of society could be this way, so that people would not feel shame in receiving a diagnosis. I think of the various diagnostic labels as nothing more than a way of naming the collection of difficulties with which patients and their families come to us. And they can truly help. For instance, if you were aware that your child was disorganised, struggled to concentrate, fidgeted and ran across roads without looking, then receiving a diagnosis of attention-deficit hyperactivity disorder (ADHD) would not change anything about the child you know and love at all. Rather, it would allow you access to reams of data and research on children like yours and information about the ways you can support them. Surely this can only be positive? The diagnosis also allows access to support structures within education, social care and the voluntary sector. As an adult, it can help self-awareness and understanding – again all positives. I would implore all who are concerned about their mental health or that of a loved one to seek assessment and support, sooner rather than later.

Our failure to understand mental health problems has been fostered by our reluctance to discuss them openly. You might argue that this statement is outdated, as over the last few years 'mental health' seems to have become all that we talk about; in October 2019, ITV paused the primetime *Britain's Got Talent* final for a minute for the sake of our 'mental health', mindfulness (or as my son described it, 'sitting in silence in an uncomfortable position') has been brought into the primary school curriculum and during the pandemic people traipsed to beaches in their thousands on 'mental health' grounds. You'd think that as a psychiatrist, I'd be dancing up and down with my pompoms shouting, 'Yay! Go Mental Health!'

But I'm not, and my outlook is fairly sombre, because some of this is simply paying lip service and shining superficial light on serious issues, which is dangerous territory. It gives the impression that something is being done and a problem is being tackled; but from what I have observed, nothing much has changed, and the stigma remains. Despite the open rhetoric on 'talking about problems', the problems we are encouraged to speak of pertain to the anxieties of 'the worried well' and there remains little appetite for talking about real, raw and violent emotions and what they can lead people to do: rubbing soil onto self-harm wounds to cause infection, having thoughts of drowning your baby, hearing voices commanding you to take your own life. No one wants to hear these kinds of thoughts and experiences; and no one is brave enough to voice them. Perhaps we consider these thoughts too extreme, 'too unreal'. We don't know what to do and that's difficult and upsetting. So we want to be protected from the realities of what mental health problems really mean. We want to think ourselves immune; but we're wrong. We all likely already know people affected by such mental health problems, and either we just don't know the full extent of them or we have chosen to turn away.* But, believe me, a mental health breakdown can happen to our friends, families, the pillars of our community. It can happen to any of us.

Pillar of a community

I was working in a busy A&E department when I met Ben. It was past 10pm when he was brought in by a member of the public. He had been begging on the streets and had burst into tears when a lady had given him change. He had started talking to her about his problems, and she had walked him to A&E. He was a 67-year-old rough sleeper and he wore the hardships of the streets. As I took the standard psychiatric history, he was swift to deny drug or alcohol abuse – perhaps too swift – but it was clear he needed to talk, and so I listened to his story, which he articulated perfectly.

Eight years ago, he had been the head teacher at a secondary school. A respected pillar of the community who had inspired teenagers for a generation. Then, he had an annus horribilis. He resigned from his job on health grounds and his wife divorced him. She got the house and he moved into a small flat. With no job, he struggled to make ends meet on his pension. He fell into rent arrears and was evicted. He had been in a hostel, but latterly had had to fend for himself on the streets. It was tough. It was cold. It was humiliating. He

---

* I know this because many of the people who are friends with both me and my husband tell me about their mental health problems, but not him, so I wonder whether I too would have remained unaware had it not been for my occupation.

couldn't take it any longer; he needed to find a way out.

He told me about his passion for teaching history, but how, the higher that he rose in teaching, the more the love of education was bled from him. He described his slow and lethal transformation from 'an inspiring teacher to a money-saving bureaucrat', until he barely recognised himself. He showed no malice that his wife had received the house in the divorce settlement. She earned it, he said. 'She did a great job with my children.' 'Children?' I exclaimed. 'Where are they now?' Bill, the eldest, was a lawyer in Edinburgh, Nicholas had moved with his young family to France and Kate, dear Kate, was a teacher in Kent with two children of her own. He spoke of his children and grandchildren fondly with evident pride in their achievements. 'Do they know you are living on the streets?' I asked. 'Surely, they would be concerned for you? Kent isn't too far away; do you think Kate could accommodate you temporarily?'

From his story, you see, I had already surmised that Ben wouldn't warrant an admission on mental health grounds. I knew that his level of distress was not at the level at which a mental health bed would be made available: he wasn't imminently about to harm himself or somebody else. If I could find a family member to take him in, it would mean I could send him to a warm home rather than back out into the dead of night with an address for the homeless shelter which he already knew.

The phone rang for a long time. It was close to midnight, so I imagined Kate and her family were already asleep. I was about to hang up, when finally, her voice came on the line. 'I'm so sorry to wake you, Mrs Anderson. My name's Dr Liang. I'm with your father in A&E.'

There was a long silence. 'What's he done now?'

Kate's story paralleled Ben's but sounded more like the

whole truth. Her father had been a long-term alcoholic. Her mother had put up with his alcoholism for longer than she should have. Kate and her brothers had watched alcohol destroy her parents' marriage and family relationships. Her brothers had washed their hands of him long ago. When he was eventually fired for turning up at his school inebriated, her mother had at last kicked him out of the house. Kate had helped her father move into a flat, buying him furniture and giving him money. But her father used the money for alcohol and sold the furniture to buy more alcohol when that ran out. She started dropping by with groceries instead, but even these were sold to fund his drinking. Rent money was used for alcohol, and not surprisingly her father was evicted. She had managed to talk him into cleaning up his act and to come to Kent to live with her; a change of scenery would allow him to start afresh. She escorted him to alcohol rehabilitation appointments, she accompanied him to AA meetings. She got him better and he moved in with her family. For perhaps six months, Ben had managed to stay on the wagon. He helped take Selina and Rothko to school. He watered Kate's garden, did the family grocery shop and took walks in the country-side. But he was restless and perhaps lonely. Slowly, but surely, the darkness set in and although Ben had first tried to hide it, it soon became evident that he was back on the liquor. The family's grocery shop became progressively more spartan as Ben siphoned money off for alcohol. The final low was when Kate came home to find the children's porcelain piggy banks smashed and raided. She asked him to leave.

This was the third phone call from A&E that Kate had received in the last 18 months. 'I can't admit him to hospital,' I said. 'I'll need to send him back out onto the street.' There was hesitation in her voice, there was concern, there was turmoil, guilt and resentment, but there was determination:

'I'm sorry. Mum and I spent the best part of our lives doing all that we could for him. I have my own family to think about now. I can't take him in.' I understood. What I had asked of her was unfair and in a way had been done to assuage my own guilt about having nothing to offer Ben myself. I scribbled the number for the alcohol service on the back of the card for the homeless shelter. He painted a forlorn figure as he walked back out onto the streets, estranged from his family and somewhat abandoned by services – and me.

The destructive power of shame

Blocking out our fears about mental illness is a natural defence mechanism to protect ourselves, but it is fear and the avoidance of it that entrenches its power (remember the CBT model where dog phobia is maintained by avoiding dogs?). The most damaging effect of the continued stigma of mental health problems is the shame that people affected come to feel. Those with mental health problems can often see themselves as defective or substandard, compounding any early-formed feelings about being 'not good enough'. People turn to hiding their problems, further socially isolating themselves and degrading their sense of belonging, at the very times when they need others' help the most. This can lead them to actively push away any support that is forthcoming. For families with loved ones suffering from mental illness, it is immensely frustrating not knowing how to help. This frustration in itself can cause relationship fractures and further isolation unless recognised and managed.

Revoekam

One of my family's lockdown Netflix addictions has been *Queer Eye*. I know that it's been around for ages, but it's the first time that I've engaged with it. The 'makeover' format has been done and re-done to death, of course, from *Pretty Woman* to the *Princess Diaries* to Gok Kwan. I have seen all of these and got the message: an eyebrow wax and a credit card can work wonders. What all of these shows have in common is the 'wow-factor' reveal. In *Queer Eye*, friends and family are intentionally kept in the dark while the protagonist experiences all manner of new positive experiences, usually involving a haircut, colourful clothes and a pep-talk. The closing scenes typically feature gasping friends and family in awe at a personal transformation from caterpillar to butterfly, ignorant of the behind-the-scenes scrubbing, scraping, validation and soul-cleansing.

Sadly, with mental illness, what we usually experience is Revoekam, or a makeover in reverse. As a friend, colleague or family member of someone with a (hidden) mental illness, what we remember is happy times with a wonderful person, then suddenly or gradually they disappear from our lives for a period, and the next time we hear about them, they are broken, destitute or dead. One minute Robin Williams was making me laugh in *Mrs Doubtfire*, making me cry in *Dead Poets Society* – and the next, he was gone. One minute I was admiring Caroline Flack and her wardrobe on *Love Island*, and suddenly she is dead. The intermittent negative life experiences and internal struggles with mental health that brought about their personal declines, often over many, many years, are shielded from us, largely because of the continued stigma of mental health problems. This is how it was when I heard about the death of our friend Chris.

Hiding in plain sight

When we met Chris for dinner on his return from travelling around Southeast Asia, it was clear that he had lost a significant amount of weight. He was still the awesome, charming, good-looking Australian we knew, but somehow, I sensed that he had become slightly smaller, in body and spirit. He told us that he had been in hospital for a year with what doctors had thought was a rare tropical disease picked up on his travels. He told us about moving back to Australia to work in his family's small business but shared little more on his life, instead focusing on asking questions about ours. At our friends' wedding, he gave a witty and well-received best-man speech but later, at the bar, Andrew noted a slight hint of resentment in his voice. This was the fifth time in the last year he'd been a groomsman, yet so far he himself had been nowhere close to having a stable relationship. As he approached his thirties, the discrepancy between how things had panned out for him compared to his peers, who were now marrying and earning 'big money' in London, seemed all the starker. This hint of dissatisfaction, paired with my sense of Chris's life having shrunk, led me to wonder if Chris may have suffered depression or had some other mental health problem. Given the lack of long-term relationships, I questioned whether he was homosexual and did not have the courage to come out; but Andrew recounted the many beautiful girlfriends of Chris's past and dismissed it.

Over the next couple of years, Australian friends whom we met from time to time would tell us about Chris when they passed through London. Lucky Chris, he's still able to party like in the good old days. He hasn't got nappies to change and noses to wipe. What no one seemed to have grasped was that the drugs and alcohol that he had used recreationally at Cambridge with his friends were becoming a more and more frequent aid, used in secret when he was on his own. Then, five years later, we heard that Chris had jumped off a cliff and died.

Mental health problems and suicide were not mentioned in Chris's obituary; it was officially reported that his actions were due to the after-effects of the rare neurological infection that he had picked up on his travels in Southeast Asia all those years ago. We asked his close friends but none of them knew whether or not he had a mental health problem, whether he was actively getting help or was struggling with his sexuality. They had seen Chris semi-regularly at the odd party, and he had 'seemed fine'. They would have surely known if Chris had been depressed, so they thought; and therefore, they were sticking to the rare tropical disease theory.

This sort of glossing-over of events perpetuates the myth that mental health problems do not beset the intelligent, talented and successful: to be a 'real' success, men in particular need to be mentally strong. And yet the denial and concealment of mental health problems only further increases barriers to support from professionals, friends and family. It is sometimes easier to believe that a friend or family member died from an unpreventable medical condition than to question the contribution of an intolerant or indifferent society; even harder to contemplate whether things may have been different if we could have reached out to talk openly about mental health.

In hindsight, Andrew remembered hearing Chris shouting at someone to get out of his dorm room late one night at university; and being surprised to find a male student in the hallway. Chris had explained that he'd been out at a party and stupidly left his dorm room unlocked and that another drunk reveller had crawled into his bed. Chris had sent him packing, and at the time Andrew had taken his explanation at face value, only thinking about it again when I repeated my theory that Chris might have been gay. I thought about the university environment of 20 years before, when the leaders of the student body refused to believe my assertion that homosexuality existed on campus. How could anyone come out in that environment? I had always held a slight grudge against Chris because of his evident surprise that Andrew and I were together. I thought he didn't like me because I was Chinese and had somehow entrapped Andrew in a world outside their sphere. Looking back now, I realise that his surprise was more directed at Andrew; that Andrew had had the courage to break free from the establishment convention and date whomever he wanted – something Chris had felt absolutely unable to do. I saw now that his reproach was not for me, but for himself. Perhaps society needs to rethink the values it seeks to promote. I am aware that this is not news – but hope that my stories can highlight the direct links between the unhealthy social values that we commonly perpetuate and mental suffering.

Out of the frying pan and into the fire

If I had had to do a risk assessment of myself when I stepped out onto the window ledge, my calculation of risk for suicide would have been low. My husband was in the house at the time, and it was an act of impulse committed in a split second of panic and desperation, a knee-jerk response to an intense sense of entrapment and suffocation. It was enough to scare me, though. The next day, I bit down hard and returned to work as if nothing had happened. But inside me, there had been a tangible change. There was a hard feeling I had deep down that the system was no longer my friend. Soon after, I did manage to secure a part-time consultant post in London in community neuropsychiatry, a service for diagnosing and helping parents support children with ADHD, autism and learning difficulties. Unfortunately, though, no sooner had I started my dream job than I had to start looking for another one, as it became evident that bullying was going to be a problem in my new workplace.

Shame and victim blaming

At my initial meeting with my line manager, he told me that as a consultant there were additional departmental roles that we had to take on outside of the advertised job plan. These service-wide roles were shared out among consultants and he had assigned me the new lead for safeguarding against child abuse. This work is critically important but challenging, depressing and stressful, and only suits people who have the experience and mental mind space to manage this, which as a working mother of two young children, I did not feel that I had at the time. Despite my explaining that I had little experience in this area and that I would prefer a role in teaching/training, he informed me that 'I would have no future in the organisation' if I did not do as I was told. I knew that I was being asked to take on the position because no one else wanted to do it, but in my view, unpopular work should be fairly shared. Therefore, I requested that the role be reviewed in two years, as my passion was for teaching. This request was also rebuffed and met with the suggestion that I was 'not a team player'. I was humbled and silenced by this – as there is nothing more guilt-inducing for wannabe 'good girls'. In shame, I got on with my additional workload as the new safeguarding lead.

It wasn't until a week later, when I introduced my colleague

Amy to my line manager, that I recognised a worrying pattern in his negotiation style. Amy was the new team manager appointed to my service. To our surprise, we were told to take on several specific high-risk patients and responsibilities, despite our concerns that our service was inappropriate to meet their needs, again on threat that if we did not, 'we would have no future in the organisation'. I wondered at how easily these words tripped off his tongue. We both tried to raise our legitimate patient concerns, but we were silenced. And with that, all semblance of control over our working lives seemed to have been removed from us. This actually turned out to be a positive experience for me, because in the past, when I had been bullied, I had always felt ashamed, believing that it was my fault in some way. In this instance, however, it was clear that this was not another personal failing because there were now two of us involved, and while I could imagine my own numerous failings, I was certain that Amy had none. It was only when Amy became subject to the same treatment as me that I saw that the shameful behaviour was not mine. The perpetrator had made the most fundamental bullying mistake. He had not isolated us and threatened us individually, which is the most successful way to bully, but he had threatened us together, giving us each a friend and ally. Afterwards, we were able to discuss our reflections of what had happened. Amy cried, and perhaps because of this, I made an informal complaint to senior management and our line manager was forced to apologise. But following that, from the system's perspective, we were clearly expected to put it behind us, and all be jolly good friends. Of course, the bullying did not cease. How can you expect bullies and victims to reconcile following a forced apology? Amy continued to be pressured to accept patients that we thought would be more appropriately managed by other services. These older teenagers were almost adults, and several had been sectioned previously and were known to forensic mental health services as individuals who were at considerable ongoing risk to themselves and others. They were, in our opinion, wholly inappropriate for a community neuropsychiatry team. Once Amy accepted the cases, I was by default clinically responsible for them. While I was no longer actively bullied, my line manager attempted to ignore me altogether, leaving me to shoulder immense risk unsupported. My own stress aside, the real victims in these political scenarios where consultants decline to collaborate are the patients.

On three days a week, I had a personal caseload of 140 patients with a high turnover, and team responsibility for over 400. Amy and I had managed to bring our new patient waiting lists down from over a year to within three months without additional resources. We were already working full-out, stretched to the limit. With the addition of high-risk patients who required high-intensity support, this workload was completely unsustainable. Neither of us felt that the desperate coping system we maintained was a healthy way to live. The day-to-day anxiety was too high; we were aware we were heading for burn-out.

Later that year, I quit my job. I had intended not to leave until I had found another job to go to, but Amy had already left because of the pressure and I couldn't 'survive' there without her. Even though I was officially unemployed – a fear of which had driven me close to the brink in the past – I was the happiest I had been in a long time. A huge weight had been lifted off my shoulders. I felt free.

I later found out that they employed a male child psychiatrist to do my old job but paid him an extra day's work to manage the same workload. Thankfully, I did not have to wait long for new employment. The paediatricians I had worked closely alongside in my community neuropsychiatry service, on hearing news of my resignation, immediately hired me on a sessional basis for 'as long as I wanted'. My spirits were boosted, as this proved to me that even if some people treated me as if I were worthless and dispensable, there were others who valued me.

Weathering adversity

Unless you are particularly charmed, your life will have many ups and downs, a veritable Tour de France. None of us can be fully insured against adversity. What we do have more control over, though, is how we respond. It's not our downfall that matters, but our next steps. Are we able to dust ourselves off and stand up again? If not, can we reach out for help to enable us to do so? Do we evade our own failings and seek to blame others, or can we reflect, learn and change? Do we persist as a damaged victim, hold grudges and seek revenge, or can we find the strength to cope, adapt and forgive; to evolve and come back stronger?

Standing back up

When a competitor reaches a valley in the Tour de France, the prospect of the next ascent must be daunting. The energy and determination required to propel themself back up a mountain is exhausting and the idea of giving up must at some point cross their mind. But at least in a cycling tour, the journey is already mapped, and it's clear in their mind that this difficult section is temporary; if they work through it, the route will become easier. In life, it's not so certain, but people who have a positive, optimistic attitude are more able to see difficulties as transitory and tend to be more resilient. When my five-year-old daughter broke her right leg falling from a climbing frame, I was more tearful than she was. I saw a perfect skeleton shattered. She looked at me crying and wiggled her left leg. 'It's OK, Mum, look – this leg's OK.' I'm so happy she has inherited her father's optimistic disposition.

For people who struggle to galvanise optimism like me, reaching out for support is important. When I lost my equilibrium, I realised that I needed to accept that my ability had limits. I had tried to be the best doctor and the best parent I could be, judging both by the highest bar, but at some point, I had to be willing to ask for help. While some people benefit from employing extra hands (nannies, tutors etc.), I went for the more economical 'review' of existing hands. Marriage is a partnership and division of labour needs to work for both parties. For a while, I had resented that my life had been turned upside down by children, while Andrew had continued just as before. My identity had changed, and I felt that it was being eroded – I was becoming someone I didn't want to be: a nagging wife, an unreliable employee. If I didn't want to lose myself altogether, I needed to fight to stay me. In a reclamation yard in Oxfordshire, some lines were redrawn, some loads lifted and some equilibrium restored. A husband/wife/partner is someone we have chosen to travel life's journey with as equals – if one person is left carrying all the bags and resentment, then the journey will likely end early.

Behavioural activation

Although I have previously mentioned that 'keeping calm and carrying on' is not the best coping mechanism because ultimately a shift at some level is required, it is true that in the short term, just continuing to engage in some activity is a good idea. In my mind, it's like treading water: it's not going to get you to the shore, but it can help you from sinking deeper under. Engagement in regular scheduled activity allows a thread of normalcy and enables some connection with the outside world to continue. Severing links with everyone and everything around you might seem like a good idea at a time when all you want to do is curl up in the foetal position, but ultimately, it will make it harder to recover as re-establishing broken links and routines is always difficult.

Choosing and committing to at least one regular activity, be it an art class, a football team or a walk with a friend, is helpful. It gives purpose to a day and ensures that at least at regular points, there is a need to get out of bed, wash, get dressed and leave the house – all positive for someone with a mental health problem. The requirement to interact with others, even if not altogether enjoyable at the time, keeps basic social skills and links alive, and who knows, may even bring comfort, pleasure and support. At the very least, other people can keep a regular eye on your mental state and call for help on your behalf if needed.

Life-long learning

In my line of work, it is fairly commonplace for me to advise parents to attend parenting courses. For some parents, this is taken as a great insult and they become very defensive and deny a need. I try to explain my reasons to them with this analogy: as a doctor it is very difficult to keep skills up to date. Thus, the General Medical Council requires all doctors to continually attend courses to update and hone skills. Attendance by no means signifies that doctors are deficient in any way; indeed, good doctors willingly apply to go on courses and train. It is often poor or struggling doctors who do not. Understanding that training and continued improvement is required is part of what makes a good doctor. This also applies to parents. It should be taken as a compliment to be asked to go on a parenting course because it means that the system believes that, fundamentally, you are a good parent – you just need the right support and tools to help you.

Mindful that we all need to keep learning and improve, I

knew that part of my recovery would come from a determination to face head on the criticisms placed at my door. I sought to improve. To address the leadership and negotiation weaknesses that had been highlighted to me, I attended the women's leadership course that had been recommended to me. When my communication skills were called into question, I willingly went on a communication course to try to improve them. When my ability to manage stress was questioned, rather than reject these concerns, I tried to make adjustments to my life to reduce anxiety and to lead a healthier lifestyle. I also strove to ensure that each step required only a little change so that it was achievable. Small and steady adjustments are more likely to amount to sustainable improvements than sudden dramatic changes.

I have learnt not to be afraid of being wrong or admit to having made mistakes in life. I have learnt that criticism can be constructive, however initially hurtful. If there is one thing that we can all be certain of, it is that we have all made mistakes and we will make many more. Trying to learn from them and do better next time will only make us stronger.

Owning your story

When I helped Leona take control of her experience of rape, she told me, 'I'm not a victim, I am Leona, I am a Lion, I am strong – this is not who I am.' And I told her to write down her story, that this would help. Although my own life challenges are incredibly trivial by comparison, workplace bullying and stress wore me down and undoubtedly affected my mental health. I started to take my own advice and wrote down my story to see if I could make sense, gain control and master my own narrative.[36] In the last two years, I have grown stronger mentally through the active process of writing down my thoughts, feelings and experiences. Early angry and vitriolic versions have been revisited, edited and refined until

I have finally been able to achieve forgiveness, understanding and validation. I know I am not the perfect daughter, sister, wife, friend, colleague, employee, parent or doctor, but I am trying to improve each day, and that is enough for me now.

PART THREE

Finding your tribe: the pros and pitfalls of belonging

8

Belonging through exclusion: the mental health impact

When Tina switched her school shoes to Doc Marten's at my grammar school in the early 90s, the whole class followed suit. Bros was the acceptable band to follow, non-existent was the desirable skirt length and Victoria was the designated child to victimise. Tina didn't even need to victimise Victoria personally; others did that for her. She merely had to laugh when people told her what had happened. To avoid being the butt of all jokes like Victoria, it was imperative that we didn't wear our skirts long like her, didn't listen to Debbie Gibson like her and that we avoided sitting with her at all costs.

One of the basest short-cuts to creating a sense of belonging is through the exclusion of others. Amazingly, social structures are so simple that the same rules apply in the playground as in the highest political arenas. At my school, denigrating group outsiders like Victoria became a short-cut for feeling like one of the gang, helping to deflect from any personal insecurities. Similarly, political leaders often encourage an 'us and them' mentality to quickly shore up group cohesion and their own positions. To do this, they need not openly advocate discriminatory laws (although some do) or even use divisive rhetoric (although some do); they simply need to tolerate discrimination or those who discriminate so that discrimination is enacted, nonetheless. What is tolerated becomes acceptable and accepted. When group identities become strengthened and the denigration of group outsiders becomes used as a tool, then group ideals can become more extreme. Group members may then demand laws that protect their own group at the expense of others: the powerful become stronger and increase their sense of belonging; the weak, the marginal and different, those who don't belong, are laid to waste, forgotten or left behind.

Many of those who are marginalised or victimised are selected on the basis of broad prejudices: race, gender, religion, sexual preference, class, disability, mental health problems or neurodiversity. They are easy targets as the differences between them and those in power are often visible and tangible. Many people, myself included, when faced with the choice between Tina and Victoria, experienced an uncomfortable conflict: to conform and preserve my own social status; or to stand with the marginalised and preserve my moral integrity. These are difficult decisions for adults, let alone children, to make. Hard as it can be to admit to oneself, 'turning a blind eye' or 'staying silent' is a strategy that all of us have used at one time or another. It is fortunate that in more recent times, with shifts in power, those traditionally marginalised are gaining in voice and impact and encouraging their peers to speak up. It will be a challenge, however, to consolidate this into real change.

Forgotten children and families

There is much made in the media about 'foreigners', 'immigrants', 'refugees' and 'asylum seekers' using up valuable public resources in health and education. What is less publicised is that it is these very groups who have little or no voice in public services and tend to get the least resource allocation with respect to need. The impact of this can only serve to perpetuate social inequality.

Jay's story is a short but depressing reflection on the status of educational inequality. Jay was referred to clinic by his school in a very deprived area of London for an attention-deficit hyperactivity disorder (ADHD) assessment. He had just turned 11 and the school was getting reports in place ready for secondary transfer. Teachers noted that Jay was working at well below the standard of his peers and wondered if ADHD was perhaps the reason for his lack of attainment; at least, that was what the referral implied. When I met Jay, he was quiet and calm, not remotely like the fidgety or restless boys I usually saw in clinic. He didn't profess boredom within minutes of arrival or start rummaging in his mother's bag for an electronic gadget. He took up the pen and paper in front of him and started to draw. His mother's English wasn't strong, and it took time and different ways of phrasing questions for me to establish an understanding with her; even then, we often required Jay's help. It reminded me of when my father was taken away in an ambulance to have his burst appendix removed and my older sister, herself only 11 years old, went with him because the paramedics needed a translator. It was unfortunate that Jay's referral had not mentioned the language barrier, as a translator could have been booked.

It is customary to start ADHD assessments by gaining an indication of a child's ability. When I asked Jay's mother about his reading, she told me that he was unable to read. He could recognise the letters of the alphabet but had not progressed beyond phonics – this, despite having been in a UK primary school since reception. Flabbergasted, I asked the mother what Jay did in class during English lessons if he was known to be unable to read. 'Oh,' his mother said, 'he go with babies.' I was shocked, but Jay confirmed that during English lessons, he would join reception class, and sit on the carpet for carpet time to learn phonics. I looked through Jay's notes for any mention of dyslexia or learning difficulties, teaching assistants, special needs provision or an educational health-care plan. There was nothing. Jay had been dutifully attending mainstream school on a daily basis from reception to almost transfer to secondary school with no additional educational support – despite full recognition from his parents and the school that he was unable to read. Clearly, the school was not willing or able to spend the resources that were due Jay, to support him individually to learn to read. I wondered how he coped on a daily basis at school; reading is required in more subjects than English, and from a rough-and-ready assessment, Jay was not so hot on numeracy either. How on earth could he access any aspect of the curriculum beyond art and PE? Sending 11-year-old children to join four-year-olds to learn to read is wholly inadequate and inappropriate, and it struck me that this would not happen in a school in a middle-class area, and that this would certainly not have happened if Jay's mother had had a strong enough grasp of English to complain about it. I understood that with austerity measures, educa-tion, like the health service, was being severely stretched, and in most cases I had a lot of sympathy for teachers who were having to make the most of what little resource they had to help their students. After all, we in mental health were doing the same; but in Jay's case, I couldn't find evidence of any redeeming factor.

Jay didn't have ADHD or any other mental health condi-tion. He was a good boy and helped his mother as much as he could, given his intellectual limitations. The sad irony is that, had Jay had behavioural problems, if he had been hitting other children, spitting at teachers and throwing furniture about, if he had attacked a four-year-old sitting next to him on the carpet, he would likely have had an educational psychology assessment years earlier. He would have been diagnosed with intellectual disability and given a place at a special needs school, but because he caused no trouble, because neither he nor his mother had a voice, his needs were neglected. Later, as an NHS consultant in a wealthy upper-middle-class setting, I couldn't help but think of Jay at times when I was being bullied by articulate, dual-professional parents to write letters to school boards demanding that their children have more time allocation in public exams on account of insignificant deficits in one or other subtest of an IQ test that they had privately undertaken. I try my best to write supportive letters for all my patients, but I am careful never to be a 'professional for hire', fully cognisant of the many children with similar or worse difficulties that remain unidentified because their parents do not have the means to buy assessment, who would end up playing on an uneven field as a result. The winners and losers in health are the same winners and losers in education.

As well as difficulties with access to services, marginalised groups suffer from structural unconscious bias. These are everyday biases based on the prevalent culture and 'social norms', and can lead to subtle, often unconscious slants in decision-making, which tend only to be detected if they are overtly pointed out. These decisions, of course, can have a life-changing impact on people at the receiving end.

As a junior doctor, I remember standing at the back of the cluster of people crowded around the hospital bed of five-year-old Adam. Adam was lying down with a thin wire holding together his spine. He had broken his neck after falling from a fifth-floor council flat window. He had been saved by the netting that had been put up by the council to break the falls of prospective suicide attempters. Adam's body, but not his head, had fit through the gaps in the netting, resulting in his having been suspended in the air by the neck until the police and ambulance arrived to cut him free.

Child psychiatrists are often called to see children like Adam who have very recently endured major life events, on the assumption that these kids must be traumatised and in need of immediate psychological support, but it is very often not the case. I believe it ought to be permitted, as part of the human condition, to experience grief, loss, adjustment, fear and failure without a parade of counsellors, psychologists and psychiatrists trailing you and putting their oar in. Many people, including children, have their own internal resources to process and recover from even serious accidents, and with the love and support of the people around them, most move on without the need for professional mental health input. Although there is an industry of professionals who may argue otherwise, there is very little evidence for the benefits of universal psychological debriefing following trauma and indeed the Cochrane review into this area recommends that 'compulsory debriefing of victims of trauma should cease'.[37] While psychiatrists know this, many other professionals are not aware of it and we still routinely get called to the bedsides of trauma victims. As I was interested in the case, I went along to hear the history and did say a brief 'hello' to Adam, but I was certainly not going to talk him through his near-death experience unless he wanted to. Instead, he talked about the kind nurses and the ward being noisy at night. He told me he was not in pain or discomfort (largely due to the copious amounts of painkillers).

Although Adam's spirits were fair given his circumstance, his notes made rather bleak reading. It was remarked that his two- and three-year-old siblings had been immediately removed into care, and it was likely that once he'd recovered, Adam would be too, a fact that had yet to be disclosed to him. On arrival at the council flat, the police had found that Adam's mother had been in the kitchen smoking cigarettes with the radio on, completely unaware that Adam was suspended by the neck outside. She had put the three children in the bedroom, the younger two in a playpen, and left them there unsupervised for at least an hour or so. She claimed that she had popped in on them periodically and everything had seemed fine. But later, Adam had climbed up furniture to reach the high window ledge, opened a window that should have been bolted by the council and had fallen out. A tragic accident. The single mother had indeed been negligent – she left her three very young children unattended, nearly costing the life of her eldest. Social care acted swiftly.

What was of interest to me, though, was that this was summer 2007, only a few months after the tragic story of Madeleine McCann's disappearance had broken and captivated the globe. In this instance, two doctors left their three children (all under the age of four years) sleeping unsupervised in a holiday apartment to have dinner in a restaurant nearby. The parents popped in periodically to check on the children and everything seemed fine, but later, it was discovered that their eldest child, three-year-old Madeleine, had been abducted. Social care did not move in to remove the younger siblings from the care of their parents. I am not saying that they should have, but what troubled me was the marked disparity in the actions taken by professionals in what were seemingly similar circumstances. I sympathise immensely with all the parents in both incidents: they suffered enormous grief and regret for their actions. But with respect to social care, I wondered if there was one rule for married, middle-class doctors and another for young single mothers.

Immigration services are another area where I have come across numerous examples of systemic inequality. The Windrush scandal highlighted the difficulties that legitimate immigrants have in demonstrating their right to stay in this country. Many people continue to dismiss 'immigrants' as an amorphous faceless horde of men climbing off insecure inflatables along the south coast, because they do not have direct contact with them. This is not the case in mental health services, where we meet many immigrants and asylum seekers. The ones I remember most are Michael and his mother.

The social worker called me about Michael before I met him. He was a ten-year-old autistic boy with severe learning difficulties who attended a special school in a deprived area. He largely did not speak, but had a few phrases that he could say and repeat. A week earlier, Michael had witnessed the horrifying death of his father while out shopping with him in the local supermarket. The social worker wanted Michael assessed for trauma (I reiterate that universal trauma debriefing has very little evidence base) as he had been close to his father. His father had picked him up from school each day and looked after him until 7pm, when his mother returned from work. We had a long waiting list at the time, and I decided it wouldn't be harmful to add Michael's name to this list, which meant it would probably be several months before we met; I would assess then if he was having any long-lasting adjustment problems regarding his father's death.

When I met Michael, he was in good spirits. He was doing well at his school, where he was well supported and well liked. His mother reported that aside from wanting to watch Formula One, something that he had done frequently with his father, Michael had not outwardly demonstrated that he missed him. Michael's mother Abi was a lean woman who was evidently educated (she pointed out the spelling mistakes in the social worker's referral letter) and spoke extremely eloquently. But the death of her partner had caused more than just grief for the family.

It transpired that Michael's father, a British citizen, had not been married to Abi; but had a wife and three daughters who lived in the suburbs and who had not known about Abi or Michael at all until shortly after his death. When they found out about them, they were shocked, could not accept them and would not meet them. Abi was originally from Sierra Leone. She had an older daughter at university there, but at some point had chosen to move to the UK with Michael to be closer to Michael's father. It seemed that Michael's father was sponsoring Abi's residence in the UK, but she had no recourse to public funds and was also not permitted to take a well-paid job as this would breach her immigration conditions, and therefore worked long hours picking up litter in the community. Their plan, as far as I could fathom, was that Michael's father would help Abi with childcare and additional money to supplement her meagre income until she had 'served her time' living in the UK and could apply for the right to remain. Once this was achieved, Abi could get a better-paid job and support Michael herself. In the meantime, Michael and Abi lived in poverty together in one bedroom of a shared lodging occupied by ten other adults. Their room consisted of not much more than a double bed and a TV.

With the death of Michael's father, Abi was left without the additional income he used to give her, and without a sponsor for her residence visa or childcare for her disabled son. She felt uncomfortable leaving ten-year-old Michael, a vulnerable child, with the various lodgers in her abode, but she had no other choice than to continue to work or be evicted and starve. Social services were already aware of this situation and the inherent risks. At the same time, Abi had concerns about her right to remain in the country: would she be thrown out now as her sponsor had died? Since Michael was the son of a British citizen, shouldn't he be eligible for citizenship? Was this possible if his father was now dead? She asked me all these questions, but I did not know any of the answers. They were all problems Abi would have to solve and manage. She held it together in a calm and collected manner until I asked: Do you miss him? For an instant, she let the tears well up, but then she checked herself and her composure was restored once more. There was too much to do, her shift picking up litter would be starting soon, and she would need to take Michael back to school.

As a child psychiatrist, I felt impotent at this point. Aside from writing a letter to social care requesting respite support for Abi, someone who could perhaps look after Michael after school, and signposting her to various charities that could potentially help financially and with legal advice, there was very little that I could do. Even then, I knew that my letters would be close to worthless. If social care had any resource to give, they would have given it already, so in need was the family. This was the first time in my entire life that I actually considered reaching into my own wallet and giving Abi any cash that I had on me. I knew that this would not be allowed, and I knew that Abi would have been too proud to accept it. But I wondered how people like Abi and Michael, living on the margins, could have any chance of preserving their own mental well-being in their precarious circumstance (I was struggling enough with parenting children without neurodevelopmental problems, with a husband and a comfortable home). I did also wonder how Michael's father had managed to hide a child he saw daily from his wife and family, and why Abi had decided to move to the UK instead of staying in Sierra Leone, where her life might have been better, given that she had an education and a daughter already at university. It occurred to me that perhaps services for children with autism and severe learning difficulties were non-existent in Sierra Leone. Would Michael have lived in a cage? Was that why she was here fighting to stay in the UK – and wouldn't we all do the same if these were our options? Abi was such a dignified and private person, I never plucked up the courage to ask her; but I suppose that I knew why she was in the UK. It was 'love' one way or another: a love for Michael and a wish that he could live his best life, or a love of Michael's father and a hope that she and Michael could have been a small part of his life; perhaps both.

First-world inequality

Given my patients' experiences of inequality, I am all too aware that my own personal experiences pale in comparison. However, I am going to describe them to demonstrate that if someone like me, who is BME but not black (I believe there is a hierarchy of skin colour discrimination) and has the privilege of a good education, experiences some difficulties, then how much worse it must be for other ethnicities and people, particularly women, from lower socio-economic groups.

After I resigned from my job, I heard of more and more women I knew leaving the broader NHS service, informally citing bullying as a reason for their departure, and I started wondering whether my experiences were systemic. The seeds of this way of thinking had been sown during the women's leadership programme that I was advised to attend by the consultant who had informed me that I was 'too forthright and assertive'.

When we broke out into workgroups and spoke of our

personal experiences, I found that I was the most content of my group. Many of my colleagues were more brow-beaten and broken than I was, having accepted work that was not their responsibility and put up with bullying (whether at work or at home) without complaint. After the course, several attendees found the strength to leave their husbands. For me, the programme was beneficial, too, in making me realise that I was alright being forthright and assertive, and finally convincing me that it was perhaps not me that needed to change.

With this new mindset, I began to look into gender and ethnicity equality literature. As this investigation was part of my own personal search for answers, I focused on literature that referred directly to my own circumstances. I share my findings with you only as a small representation of likely much wider systemic problems in broader society.

Most people are aware of the gender pay gap problems within the BBC, where two thirds of the highest earners (salaries over £150k) on the talent side are male. Less well publicised is the fact that this pay gap is probably commonplace in every institution and sector in the land.[38] In the NHS, two in three consultants are men (despite the workforce within the NHS as a whole being predominantly female – 67%), and male doctors earn £1.17 for every £1 earned by a female doctor. There is a gender pay gap in medical bonuses (clinical excellence awards) of 51%. In the legal profession, the mean gender pay gap in 2018 was 12.7% on pay and 34.4% on bonuses, although the bonus pay gap was narrowed in 2019. The average gender pay gap in the financial sector is 23.1%, with the average gap between male and female banking bonuses being 37.7%. I have no doubt that pay gaps are significantly worse in other professions and industries, such as teaching, hospitality and factory work, which are less likely to be scrutinised.

With regards to ethnicity data in my profession, the median

basic pay for white NHS consultants is 4.9% higher than for BME consultants. This was equivalent to additional basic pay in December 2017 of about £4,644 a year more for white consultants. As a female BME consultant, I was probably afflicted with a double-whammy pay gap, but what perturbed me more than this was the growing evidence I found of racism in medicine in general. So rife is racial inequality in health that in February 2020 the *British Medical Journal* dedicated a whole issue to it – i.e. even before the spotlight of inequality was shone on BME healthcare workers by their excess death from Covid-19. Among UK graduates, 72% of ethnic minority junior doctors applying for a speciality training programme succeed on their first attempt, compared to 81% of their white colleagues. In 2016, UK-trained doctors from an ethnic minority background applying for consultant posts were less likely to be short-listed (66% vs 80%) and less likely to be offered a post than white doctors (57% vs 77%).[39]

No doctor could escape the high-profile case of Dr Hadiza Bawa-Garba, a junior doctor who was convicted of manslaughter and struck off the medical register for honest mistakes made in an understaffed hospital. She was later reinstated to the register on appeal. Many wondered whether she would have been convicted of manslaughter and struck off had she been a white male; certainly, Harold Shipman managed to kill three women between the time the first concerns were raised about his excess patient deaths and that of his arrest, and the General Medical Council only struck him off the medical register ten days after his conviction for the murder of 15 people. The data is clear: ethnic minority doctors are twice as likely to be referred to the General Medical Council and more likely to be struck off than their white counterparts. They report more workplace discrimination and bullying and there are still some reports of patients refusing to be seen by

'black doctors'.* And let us not forget the Windrush generation of healthcare professionals whose children were recently
being deported from our shores.

It was a relief for me to finally see in black and white
that I was not alone. I felt as if I had been 'unblinded', as I
had when I worked on the drug trial and sensed what was
happening but had to wait till the moment of reveal to be
sure. For so long I had beat up on myself about the failings
in my personality: not clever enough, not eloquent enough,
too hesitant, too forthright, not a natural leader, not teaching-
hospital-consultant material. I had become a diminutive and
anxious version of myself, filled with self-doubt – a far cry from
the teenager who had once confidently said 'Hmpff, I can do
that' about getting into Cambridge to study medicine. Being
enlightened to the fact that this was a common experience
for women, particularly BME women, led me to reflect on
other 'failures' in my career which had eroded my youthful
confidence and fostered within me shame and the sense that
I was not good enough. I began to wonder if they too were
influenced by the unthinkable: systemic prejudice, something
that I had been led to believe had died with Stephen Lawrence.

Do you remember that right at the start of my story I
mentioned my highly enjoyable BA research project on musical
mood induction? Well, this happened to be my second-choice
BA research project. My first-choice project had been with the
same supervisor, but to study video mood induction. This was
a bigger and more significant project, and was given to a white
male student whom I didn't really know. The research project

---

* Just in case there is any confusion about who 'black doctors' are, I recall
a conversation between a patient of mine and her husband: 'Which one's
your doctor?' he asked. 'The black one,' she replied, referring to me. 'Oh,
they are all black these days,' commented her husband. In that particular
hospital, there were no doctors of African/British African/Caribbean
origin, although there were many Asian doctors.

allocations were determined purely by CV and so I naturally figured his CV must just have been better than mine and that one just had to accept these little failures in life, acknowledge one's own inadequacies and move on, which is what I did. Later though, I was told by my supervisor that he regretted not having awarded that bigger project to me because the white male had turned out to be less than committed and had barely managed to complete it. I can't help but wonder if it had anything to do with my being an ethnic minority female, evident by my weird name and stated gender, as I knew my CV was strong.

Research has shown that there is unconscious gender bias in the processing of CVs. In a Yale University study, when a researcher submitted identical CVs for two fictitious candidates – one male and one female – to various professors for a position as laboratory manager, male and female professors alike preferred the male candidate's CV and were willing to pay the male candidate a higher salary. Similar experiments have been undertaken for males with white- and ethnic-sounding names; the candidates with white-sounding names received preference.[40]

In a previous chapter, I mentioned that I won a research prize for the work that I did on suicide in Cape Town. What I omitted to mention then was that following my submission for consideration for the prize, I received an email from the judging committee asking me to provide the email address of my supervisor so that he could confirm that the paper was authored by me. At the time, I presumed this was standard procedure, although my supervisor in South Africa found it unusual. It was only later, when I supervised a white trainee to write a paper that won a research prize and was not contacted to confirm authorship, that I realised this was not standard practice. Later, at the prize-giving lunch for my award, I sat among a clutch of six white male professors. None of them spoke to me, let alone asked me about my research. It was an excruciating hour, being wholeheartedly ignored at the lunch that was held supposedly in my honour. I figured that there was something wrong with me. That I was no good at social-ising or conversation, that I was uninteresting or boring. I felt utterly wretched and humiliated, and I couldn't wait to get out of there. That evening, my husband suggested we go out to celebrate my award, but I had no appetite. I didn't even dare tell him what had happened, but just said the prize was no big deal. Later, when I was shortlisted for interview for a prestigious PhD fellowship, my heart sank when I walked into the interview to find the panel consisted wholly of those same lunch dates. At least it came as no surprise that I did not get the fellowship, which was awarded to a white male.

I have also told you about my joy at being made a clinical lecturer after my fourth research paper was published in a peer-reviewed journal. Well, what I didn't tell you then was that my application was initially rejected. I had researched the very clear criteria on the website prior to applying and had felt that they had all been met; and so, I was a little ashamed when I received the 'We regret…' letter. The shame was directed at my own arrogance that I should have applied in the first place. 'Who did I think I was?' said the voice inside my head. Later, I mentioned the failure to Professor Carmichael, who was my supervisor at the time. She was outraged as she knew that I met all the specified criteria. She asked to see my letter and within a week, I received another letter which awarded me clinical lecturer status. The trouble was that by then, it didn't feel like a proud accomplishment. I didn't celebrate becoming a clinical lecturer; instead I was ashamed and constantly ques-tioned if I was deserving.

Recently, I found a research article that looked at fellowship awards granted by the Medical Research Council of Sweden.[41] They found that female candidates needed substantially more publications to achieve the same recognition rating as men and needed to be 2.5 times as productive as the average male applicant in order to receive the same competence score, unless they personally knew someone on the selection panel. It seemed that I had been one of the lucky ones; although I didn't know anyone on the selection panel, Professor Carmichael had been willing to challenge the panel on my behalf. What of the many other women who have applied for positions like this without a champion?

The realisation of what was probably the worst betrayal in my work-life experience came out of the blue at a Royal College conference only a few years ago. An eminent contemporary colleague of mine, highly intelligent, articulate and good-looking, was giving his swansong lecture before heading out to a new professorship in the US. He had been six months behind me in training and a rising star from the outset, and I didn't for one moment begrudge all the good things that happened to him. In his speech, he gave the utmost thanks to Professor Townsend, our old head of child psychiatry. His words came as a 'mirror crack'd from side-to-side' moment for me: 'I have Professor Townsend to thank for my amazing career,' he said. 'I can still remember the day at the very start of my training, when I cautiously knocked on the door to Professor Townsend's office and told him about my passion to study adolescent depression. He gave me some data that was to be the start of my research career, in which he has mentored and guided me every step of the way. I am entirely grateful as I would certainly not be here without him.' My heart and breathing stopped and I literally felt faint as I flashed back to my own earnest youth and the reality dawned on me.

From my calculations, the described scene must have

happened six months after I had cautiously knocked on the same door at the start of my training and stated my same passion for adolescent depression. Rather than gaining a lifetime of mentorship, I had been told to go and knock on someone else's door. Perhaps I didn't express my passion ardently enough, perhaps I was not as articulate. Perhaps my Cambridge degree and small clutch of publications from South Africa wasn't good enough.* Or perhaps, perhaps, some of us just don't get an equal opportunity? We don't belong in the club.

For most of us who are not invited, or do not even know about the existence of Slughorn's Slug Club,** finding out about its existence can come as a slap in the face, as it did for me. What hurt me most was that Professor Townsend had always been kind to me and up until that moment I had no inkling that he had denied me mentorship from the very beginning of my career. In many industries there are senior men whose opinions are highly valued, they are often 'kingmakers' in the field and who they endorse is important, but it can be a problem if they are just that: never making queens. I thought about the many other women that there must be struggling to progress in all manner of male-dominated professions. Even now, they likely believe, as I did, that we were just not as good as those men, all along unaware, as I was, that those men were being given more opportunities, endorsement and support by seniors whom we considered fair and sympathetic. I realised how difficult it was to fight against something you didn't even know existed.

---

* The degree was unlikely a problem as the professor and I had studied exactly the same courses at the same university.

** Professor Horace Slughorn from the Harry Potter books was famous for favouring particular students (girls based on talent, like Hermione Granger, and boys based on who their parents were, like Harry Potter), whom he invited to join his elite Slug Club.

Following my 'unblinding', I developed a new zeal for talking about my experiences to others, and in turn, they shared their experiences with me. Senior women I respected and admired in my industry told me of being side-lined in favour of male colleagues. At least six male colleagues I trained with are now professors, whereas only one female colleague became one and had to move abroad to achieve this. I now believe that sexism and racism, conscious and particularly unconscious, are pervasive in all UK institutions. If they exist in the low-profile, low-prestige, ostensibly 'female-friendly', definitely female-dominated speciality of child psychiatry, then what of women in competitive high-profile sectors such as academia, surgery, law, banking, the media and politics? What heightened inequalities must exist there? If well-educated and assertive women have been unable to make headway in these sectors, what of less-educated and less-assertive women in other employment sectors?

An additional revelation to me was that in my career, inequality had started way earlier than motherhood; all the experiences that I have just described happened to me before I had children. Contrary to my assumptions, and the socially encouraged narrative, it was not my decisions about parenthood that had caused the demise of my career trajectory. I also realised that I wasn't the only one who been lulled into believing that gender inequality no longer existed. I remembered the conversations that I had had with my talented friends in my early twenties – a friend in the banking sector talking about her lovely team which was made up of exactly 50:50 men and women. 'Who said banking was sexist?' she told us. We all congratulated ourselves for having been born at an optimal moment for gender equality. But then, following the bust of the dot.com bubble, when there was a round of redundancies, it was all the women in the bank save for my friend who were gone. All the men had survived. She described the subsequent environment as miserable; she was frequently being mistaken for the PA. There are countless more stories of this kind.

In addition to discrimination, many women continue to experience direct harassment in the workplace, a further hindrance to their careers. We already know that female politicians receive more death and rape threats than their male counterparts, but even more remarkable is that everyone I know has either a personal harassment story to tell or knows someone directly affected by it. A lawyer friend reported to me how as a trainee she had to climb out of the bathroom window of a fancy restaurant in the City to escape the predatory advances of an important client. When she reported the incident to her colleagues, they laughed and chastised her 'for getting herself into a compromising position which may have cost them a client'. A trainee surgeon friend was openly and repeatedly reproached for 'being the first trainee in history to dare to request a second round of maternity leave in a highly sought-after surgery training programme'; she was so distraught that she miscarried at 16 weeks.

Add race to the mix and we get more stories. My husband's black female colleague resigned from the company a few weeks after an office party where a company director had asked her for more hors d'oeuvres, mistaking her for a waitress. My black barrister friend told me about attempts to usher her out of a meeting because it was only for legal counsel and not defend-ants. Many people like me have wondered about our treatment at the hands of the white establishment, but we so wanted to belong that we ultimately bought the 'honest mistake' argu-ments we were given as explanations – but should we have done?

Can we move forward?

There are so many subtle ways in which people in positions of power and influence push for the acceptance of the status quo, for instance signalling that individuals, not systems or society, are to blame for their own fates and are being oversensitive when they object to remarks such as: 'He was just being friendly, he's a naturally tactile guy' or 'Don't be daft, it was a joke; she's got lots of black friends' or 'There are too many immigrants in this country... but not you, you're different, you're one of the good ones'. From women having concerns about gender discrimination being dismissed outright because 'two senior positions are held by women, so it can't be true'* and rape victims being asked if they were drunk or wearing a short skirt, to most recently, in the context of rising Covid cases, BME communities being patronised with comments about their 'multi-generational living arrangements'. It is perhaps because these narratives are so mainstream that each and every one of us at some level buys into them and perpetuates the cycle.

On top of this, there is a lethal strategy of reassurance, procrastination and inaction. I have been to so many 'women in science' events, and each has made me more cynical. At one event organised to promote retention of women in science, I was hit by the irony that it was being chaired by Amelia, my Sun and Doves colleague who had been a rising star in adult psychiatry. I had caught up with her a year earlier at a meeting where she'd told me that she had left academic psychiatry and the NHS due to workplace bullying and subsequent clinical depression. It seemed perverse that she had now been recruited to encourage women to stay in the discipline that she herself

---

* By this argument there should be no racism in the USA because Barack Obama was able to become president.

had found toxic to her mental health. I have stopped going to equality events of this kind. I came to realise that they were PR machines rather than agents of real change: we take your concerns seriously, so much so that we will run promotional events, we will tick boxes and obtain 'Equality Certificates' to put on our websites. Perhaps, if you insist on making a fuss, we will launch an inquiry. We will review the inquiry recommendations. We'll do something about it soon. Soon-ish.

My worry is that the current flurry of activity with regards to race equality will follow the same trajectory of lip service and procrastination. There is much earnest talk and consternation, but very little concrete change. There appears to be a disconnect between public will and political will. It is clear that it is time for tangible actions, and on a personal level there are things that we can all do to help.

Promoting inclusion

We know that a feeling of belonging is beneficial for people's mental health. Children who feel they belong in their families are happier; children who feel they belong in their school are much more likely to achieve; adults who have a sense of belonging in their workplace are more productive; and people who feel they belong in their community and country are more content, altruistic, socially minded and healthier. Why then does society not promote inclusion at all levels? If we are truly interested in the mental health of our friends and family, we need to consider societal inclusion, even more so if we are in positions of secure belonging and have the power to influence change. Even if we feel powerless to change laws and national policy, we are all part of society and how each and every one of us behaves influences other people day to day.

Belonging at home

For me, parenting is the most important job in the world. If we instil our belonging beliefs and values in our children, our ideas will last long after we are gone. Think about it: who at your workplace will remember your excellent PowerPoint presentations and leadership strategies a year or two after your retirement? Yet, your children will remember your every action or inaction. Your values will be enacted day to day by your children and by their children and the generations that follow, affecting the people around them and society at large.

Helping our children to understand and accept themselves and encouraging them to be authentic in a world of fake social media is a challenge, but one that we must face head on. Advising our children to seek out others so that they can belong is protective for their future mental health. Teaching them to be open and inclusive helps them make friends and helps other children to also feel that they belong. From a child psychiatrist's perspective, a happy home life can significantly mitigate the negative effects of biology and genetics, in terms of both success and mental health. Indeed, recent child mental health surveys show that children in families with healthy family functioning have almost five times fewer mental health problems.[42]

Belonging in schools

School life is a significant part of our childhood, and so can also contribute to positive or negative life experiences, which shape the developing brain. Inclusive, supportive and nurturing schools produce children with higher self-esteem and fewer challenging behaviours. We should all champion these values in schools – and not just by talking the talk. Being inclusive entails doing things which do not come naturally to us, such as being supportive and understanding of children who may display challenging behaviour, rather than condemning them as troublemakers. School exclusions have increased dramatically with austerity, fuelling division and a sense of lack of belonging in a whole generation.[43] We therefore have a situation where, even while politicians are advocating the importance of children's mental health, some of their policies are detrimental to it. They proudly declare more money for school counsellors, but in many cases it is the reduction in the number of teaching assistants, the increase in class sizes and severe cuts in special educational needs provision that contributed to the mental health struggles of children in the first place. It is a nonsense to provide a plaster while exacerbating the wound.

Belonging is good for business

An article entitled 'The Value of Belonging at Work' in the Harvard Business Review stated that 'if workers feel like they belong, companies reap substantial bottom-line benefits.' High belonging was linked to a whopping 56% increase in job performance, a 50% drop in turnover risk and a 75% reduction in sick days. 'For a 10,000-person company, this would result in annual savings of more than $52M… In contrast, it has been shown that work-place exclusion leads to team (and self-) sabotage.'[44] Many companies have been working on increasing diversity to help with workplace inclusion; however, support of diversity needs to be followed through so that talent is retained and is not a mere tick-box exercise. Workplaces need not only to be seen to be representative of the staff, but to be fair, a place where people are treated with respect and valued for what they bring. If you have any power in the organisation in which you work, remember that your employees are human beings and their thoughts, contributions and feelings matter. They need to feel like they belong to something they value, and have faith in the system in order to remain committed and give their best.

Belonging in our communities

One of the worst feelings I felt in my darkest times was of being rejected and silenced, and part of my recovery involved learning to use my voice again. Initially, this was just moaning about my woes to friends and colleagues, but later I began to reach out to anyone who would listen through a blog and now, with this book, I hope to promote as best I can the basic need for people to be loved by their family and respected in their school, work and community. My contribution to change is small, but its benefits for my own well-being have been immense. Giving light to the experiences of my patients, speaking and sharing my truths and finding others with similar stories in all walks of life has finally made me feel that I belong. It is no wonder that social prescribing has become increasingly popular; it makes sense – giving back to the community is a win-win situation. Communities benefit from the contributions of their members and people giving back get a great sense of well-being from their increased connectedness with those around them. I realise that not everyone is able to commit large amounts of time to serving the community, but small acts, such as empowering, encouraging and validating others, even within your own work and social sphere, is enough. For women in particular, never underestimate the power of a well-timed 'You've got this' and a congratulatory 'Girl, you rock'. And of course, you can also vote.

I don't wish to get overly political, but we live in times when it feels as if the concepts of family and community have been undervalued, where media and politicians have contrived to divide people for their own ends. Ultimately, I hope that I have conveyed that mental health goes beyond personal genetics, psychology and responsibility, to embrace wider issues of poverty, inequality and thwarted life opportunity in society. Without a doubt, the government's decade-long pursuit of austerity has led to a fall in national and potentially generational well-being. With the likelihood of further global economic gloom to come, future governments need to make considered choices to focus on repairing the key services of health, mental health, education and social care. Meanwhile, society needs to think about nurturing kindness and coming together rather than further division. Without these wider changes, any mental health policy will be ineffectual.

9

Belonging through acceptance: a way forward

I have mentioned several times in previous chapters that my own sense of belonging was heightened during arduous medical training by the support of fellow junior doctors who were enduring the same hardships. Feeling a shared sense of adversity or purpose can foster an immense sense of unity and connection. So strong is this sense of belonging that population depression and suicide rates dropped during the two world wars. It is no surprise that during the Covid-19 pandemic, communities, workplaces, families and neighbours have come together more than could have possibly been imagined just a year ago, with many people reporting a greater sense of belonging in their lives, sometimes having spoken to their neighbours for the very first time.

My sister could not have got through her experience of cancer without her cancer support group, and I could not have got through maternity leave without the support of my NCT buddies. Time and time again in the mental health services I have led, the support groups that we have encouraged families to set up have often been what has made the most difference to them. Sometimes, what we need more than a professional opinion is the nod of affirmation from someone who has been there, experienced exactly what we have been through and who can give us their time, a hug of understanding, a mug of tea and a shoulder to cry on. I think that if everyone had access to this, the world would be a much happier place.

So, what are the obstacles to this kind of society? How can we break through superficial divisions and come to a world where belonging is achieved by the acceptance and understanding of others? In my parenting book *Inside-Out Parenting*, I emphasise the importance of accepting children for who they are, however they differ from our expectations as parents. This fosters their sense of belonging and strengthens their feeling of security and well-being. What if we could do this for society at large? Foster a society that embraces diversity, is curious to understand others and celebrates the fact that everyone has something different but valuable to offer. One that understands that, despite diversity of appearance, wealth, class, ability and opinion, fundamentally, we are all the same – people looking for warmth, love and understanding.

Supportive environment matters

Oscar's parents were awake to this from the get-go. They were quick to appreciate and accept everything about him and use their own resources to ensure that there was a supportive and understanding place for him in society.

Oscar was a 13-year-old boy with ADHD. He was adopted by Dan and Viv at the age of three, and by the time that I saw him in clinic with his dad, he had already been doing well on stimulant medication for a few years. He was on my list of routine follow-up cases who were only reviewed once or twice a year. What made Oscar and his dad so memorable was a conversation we had about Oscar's future. Dan told me that, although Oscar was doing well emotionally and behaviourally, they were aware that his mild learning difficulty meant that he still had academic limitations. He was a sensitive boy, who was polite and caring, but he would need a kind and perceptive employer to get the best from him, otherwise he would likely withdraw and break down. Knowing their son well, Dan was not going to take any chances. 'Don't worry, doc,' said Dan, 'we've already thought of that. He's going to join me in my business, so we can look after him. He's really good at doing things if we tell him exactly what to do, and I know that he won't mess me about.' Dan owned a small construction company and had started Oscar on odd jobs under his supervision. It was heart-warming to know that Oscar would always belong in his family and in the family company, giving him a place in society. As well as making use of his ability, earning money and being independent, he could develop a sense of purpose, contribute to the community and gain self-respect. His weaknesses were accepted, supported and ameliorated; his strengths were treasured.

Since Oscar, I have seen and heard about several families who have adapted or even set up their own companies to incorporate a worthwhile role for their children with special needs. I know that not many families have the power to do this, but it's an example of how the environment they live in can make a big difference in outcomes for children with neurodevelopmental difficulties. If more people, particularly those with power, invested in special needs and disability employment, they would gain hard-working and loyal employees who could make a meaningful contribution to society.

Peter was another child whose parents had taken the initiative to support him. He was a 14-year-old boy from Romania, whose family had recently moved to the UK. Peter was remarkably large for his age. He was almost six feet tall and was overweight, largely because of the considerable amounts of anti-psychotic medication that he had been taking since the age of four. He had a diagnosis of ADHD, ASD and intellectual disability. Although he was able to speak, he only said a few phrases and was functioning at the level of a four-year-old rather than a 14-year-old. He needed help and supervision with all aspects of his care, but this was becoming increasingly difficult due to his size and strength. Both Peter's parents were frank in admitting that they had explicitly looked for work in the UK as they had heard of the excellent national healthcare available here. Unfortunately, I was to disappoint them, something they repeatedly reminded me of when I would not give into their demands to increase Peter's medication.

With careful persuasion, I actually managed to switch his medication to one that was half the strength of his old one, and for well over a year, this worked well for both Peter and his family. Because of this, I built a solid relationship of trust with them, despite their initial grievances with me. Unfortunately, though, as Peter grew, he became stronger and more challenging. When he did not get his own way, he started hitting his grandmother, who looked after him while his parents worked. And it wasn't long before Peter's mother was also overwhelmed by the burden of care. Peter's outbursts were no different from the tantrums of any other child functioning at the level of a four-year-old, but because of his build, it was not possible for his female relatives to contain him.

I started to have the difficult but inevitable conversations with the family about residential schooling. The family were in floods of tears as they loved Peter and wanted him to stay with the family. Residential placements are often far from a child's home, and Peter's family were reluctant to consider this at all. At each clinic visit, I observed the cuts and bruises that Peter was inflicting on his mother, but I was running out of ideas. As their next appointment approached, I had steeled myself to have a stern word with the family again, thinking that I would need to insist on residential care options in view of safeguarding concerns for both Peter and his mother. I had previously had another mother of a teenage patient with ASD, ADHD and intellectual disability resort to calling the police to stop her son attacking her. The last vision the mother had of her mentally unwell son was of him being handcuffed and pushed into a police van before being sent to a mental health facility in the north of England – horrifying for any parent. I really did not want this to happen to Peter.

But when I saw the family next, they were all smiles. With them stood a six-foot-three young man with a warm smile, built like a brick house. 'This is Ivan,' Mum said. 'He is a nurse from Romania, and he has come to live with us to help us with Peter.' I think it is basic human instinct to behave better in the presence of physical dominance. Even the most impulsive of us would likely reconsider striking out in front of Tyson Fury or the like. Peter was delighted with his new companion, who was able to block his lashing out when it occurred.

I couldn't help thinking that this was the humane version of the Taiwanese boy's cage. A way of allowing Peter to continue to engage with the world, while preventing him from hurting himself or others. In special needs schools and residential facilities, appropriate staffing levels are highly correlated with the absence of challenging behaviour. Yes, I could see how one kind but physically massive person, like Ivan, could fulfil the same task. It was likely that Peter would eventually need a residential placement, but if Ivan's presence could allow him to stay with his family for even a year longer, that would mean a lot to them.

In the end, the best solution, as so often in my view, was not medical but environmental: providing appropriate supportive environments for people to allow them to be their best selves, to stay with the people they love and feel a sense of belonging.

This really hurts

I could perhaps have ended my personal story at this point, unshackled from a job that wore me down and soon to find a better one. I had had my crisis-point life wobble, but I had reset my direction and found my new freedom and happy-ever-after. But this would have avoided addressing the main point about life that differs from fairy tales – it marches on beyond the artificial happy ending. Mental health is not a bank that we can draw from continually without consequence. It is perhaps impossible to have my anxious nature, absorb stress from patients, do front line clinical work, take on the demands of research, service management, office politics and bullying, listen to depressing national and global politics, be there for school pick-ups, drop-offs, class assemblies, packed lunches, ballet, football, piano, children's friendship problems, children's accidents, ageing parents, family health problems, friends with mental health problems, friends' children with mental health problems and husband's work problems without a fall-out. And unbeknownst to me at the time, a literal fall-out was about to happen.

I had been having some tooth sensitivity for a while, but neglected to do anything about it as I had so much going on in my life. By the time I went to the dentist, it really hurt. I was told that I had severe cracking in several teeth from a life-time of stress grinding. I was to lose a tooth and required root canal treatment in several others. This was extremely disheartening for a life-long, caries-avoidant, diligent tooth-brusher.

The dentist asked me about the stress in my life and urged me to take anti-depressants. I thought about all the times in my life when I had literally got through painful situations by gritting my teeth, clenching my jaw and biting down hard. It had finally taken its toll. This time, I fell into a heap and cried.

I should have known better than others that stress (whether it be from bullying, bereavement, break-ups or just everyday bullsh*t in our life) is not something we can 'cheat'. It needs to be acknowledged, tackled and processed, or one way or another it will take its toll psychologically or physically. In my case, although I had been able, most of the time, to avoid a psychological fall-out, the effort of absorbing the stress in my life had had to manifest itself somewhere – in this case, in my mouth. The thought of sucking up roast dinners through a straw was what finally prompted me to evaluate my own case objectively. I had the breakthrough realisation that being understood and accepted by others only comes from under-standing and accepting ourselves. A true sense of belonging is not possible unless we firstly and foremostly accept ourselves and our limitations. For most of us, myself included, this is the hardest step of all in the path to belonging, and one which we all try to avoid.

Yet it is the most important step. Only then can we be confident enough to present our authentic self to others and show people who we really are. Their response can help us accurately gauge which of them are truly supportive, and the right people with which to nurture a deeper and more mean-ingful relationship. This process sounds simple, but in fact, being willing to look at yourself so objectively can take a lot of hard work, which is why many people struggle even to begin on the path of true belonging.

Understanding yourself

Without exception, the hardest part is being willing to understand and accept yourself, warts and all. As we saw with Ginny, Chris and so many others, avoiding or denying 'the difficult' might seem like the easier course; but ultimately not facing up to ourselves, to our story, who we really are, makes it very hard for us to ever belong. Most people are able to change or adapt to new environments; this is a positive, as it allows us to 'fit in' in new situations. However, it is also true that if we do this too much, we can lose sight of who we are and suffer mental health consequences too. The cognitive dissonance (the stress of holding two opposing values or beliefs) inherent in being everything to everyone is corrosive. In these situations, although we might find a superficial sense of belonging, it can never be satisfactory as we cannot be sure whether others like us for who we really are, or for who we are pretending to be. This causes a fundamental sense of insecurity about whether we actually belong or not.

Understanding ourselves takes soul searching, honesty and forgiveness. Some people, in order to know themselves better and forgive themselves, need to make sense of why they are the way they are. However, while we need to try and learn from the past, continually dwelling on it can be detrimental. Personally, I think it is easier to understand and forgive ourselves if we accept that no one is perfect and that all weaknesses, whatever the cause, can be worked on.

In my parenting book, I talked about the importance of a 'growth mindset' in children, but I now think that having it is beneficial for adults too. Growth mindset is a concept pioneered by Stanford professor Carol Dweck, based on her studies of how to help children succeed.[45] Carol's theory posited that children who were praised for effort ('Well done for trying so hard') tended to challenge themselves more and ended up doing better than children who were praised for innate ability ('You're so clever'). Children who had been told that they were smart tended not to want to challenge themselves for fear of failure, whereas the children who were praised for effort developed motivation and an understanding that working led to self-improvement. Carol explains to children that the brain is like a muscle and the more you use it, the stronger it becomes. If this idea of a dynamic and plastic brain can improve our mental ability, surely it can also apply to other brain functions such as our psychology, identity and sense of self. If we are able to comprehend that none of us are the final versions of ourselves and change is always possible, then identifying weaknesses becomes a positive activity, as only by doing this can we improve and ultimately become stronger. Turning a blind eye to our weak spots, on the other hand, only leads to greater weakness.

Before starting, it is important to stress that self-awareness starts with honesty. This is only possible if you are willing to be kind and forgiving towards yourself because mistakes and behaviours that are difficult to own are part of being human. However, we tend to judge ourselves more harshly than we would judge others, so it is important to practise treating ourselves as we would a friend. Think about if a friend behaved in the way you did – how would you view it, and what would you say to them? With this more generous attitude, start making lists of your strengths and weaknesses so that your thoughts are focused and tangible.

For each weakness on your list, for instance 'not kind enough' or 'worry too much', first evaluate whether the statement is true or biased by the way you view or value yourself – if you are not sure ask honest opinions of those who care about you. If you determine the weakness to be real and important, think about possible avenues for change and improvement and write them alongside so that you have a resulting list of positive actions. Look again at your list of positive actions and where possible, break them down into manageable bite-size steps. For instance, the vague but important goal of 'become a kinder person' can be broken down into more pragmatic small steps that can be easily taken, for instance:

1. Smile and say 'Hello' to five people a week that I would normally ignore.
2. Call one family member/one friend every week 'just to say hello'.
3. Smile and say 'Thank you' and take an interest in one person a week who has done something for you, for example the office cleaner, the barista at your coffee shop.
4. Offer to help someone once a week, for example, to babysit for a neighbour who may need a break, or give a colleague a lift to work.

Small steps are more likely to be sustained and incorporated into everyday life than big changes, and can make a lot more difference than many failed attempts at grander ambitions. In the 'being kinder' scenario, you will quickly find that the positive act of being kind to others means that you also notice other people reciprocating kindness to you. It always surprises me, although it is obvious and it shouldn't, but when I smile and say 'Hello' to people, they smile and say 'Hello' back. By acting with compassion, we invite others to treat us with consideration, respect and generosity.

For the weakness of 'worry too much', first you need to identify your fears, and then it becomes easier: the standard treatment is to face them gradually (exposure and response prevention – see Chapter 2). List out your fears in order of most severe to least severe. So, for instance, for someone with social anxiety, it may look something like this:

1. Singing to a public audience.
2. Giving a speech in public.
3. Singing to close family members.
4. Giving a speech to close family members.
5. Stopping and asking a stranger for directions.
6. Asking a familiar barista for a napkin.
7. Paying for something in a shop.

There are no prizes for guessing that the next task is to then attempt to carry out each item on the list, starting with the easiest and working towards the hardest. If the jumps between each step seem too challenging, put more steps in. Enlist a friend or family member to support you with each challenge. Once you have managed to complete a step, keep repeating it until you don't feel anxious about it at all before considering the next one. This may involve acquiring a large collection of napkins, but that's OK.

Dealing with 'mental clutter'

Writing out pragmatic steps for change works for everyday problems as well as for self-improvement. Often people fall at the first hurdle of self-help because they are overwhelmed by a mass of intertangled thoughts and emotions. By setting things down on paper, you will make it easier to separate and make sense of them, because once problems are written out, they become tangible and manageable rather than overwhelming.

As a parent, I have an almost daily battle with the laundry.

Sometimes after a holiday, the mounds and mounds of dirty laundry that build up in and around the area of the laundry basket are very, very, daunting. There have been many occasions when I have just chucked the whole lot into the downstairs toilet and shut the door so that I don't have to look at it or deal with it. The problem with this is that more and more laundry is constantly being generated, and if I continue to throw it into this room, the problem becomes bigger and more daunting. The only solution is to summon up the courage to go into that room and begin the arduous and tedious process of sorting it. Washing it in batches, pairing up socks, folding up articles of clothing and putting them away one by one. This job is time-consuming, but once started there is a great sense of satisfaction in doing it, and you can see that little by little, order can be brought to even the largest and most insurmountable chaos. Try to take the same approach with the confusion of thoughts in your head and emotions in your heart. Start to write down the things that you want to work on, prioritise them and problem-solve each one; and you will begin to Maria Kondo* your mind.

As an example of a starting point, take a pen and a piece of paper and create two lists:

1. Make a list of your goals, hopes and dreams and the time that you spend working on making them happen.
2. Make a list of relationships that you have and the time you spend talking to each person about their feelings and experiences.

The next task is to sort and prioritise your lists. It is helpful to write the items on your lists on post-it notes so that you can move them around to consider their priority. Arrange the

---

* See her book, *The Life-Changing Magic of Tidying Up*, for more on this.

lists so that you have absolute clarity for yourself about the relationships that really matter and those that don't, the ambitions that are most important to you, and those that would be nice but which are not make-or-break. The process of thinking carefully about priorities is therapeutic if in doing so you also think about whether your time and mental energy is being optimally directed. It allows you to see and redress any imbalances you find between where you are spending your resource and what is actually important to you. For example, you might realise that you are spending a lot of time worrying about the judgement of someone who is not even significant in your life; or that you are spending so much time and energy in a job that was meant to 'tide you over' that you have not been able to move forward on your passion project.

Once you are clear about your priorities, take the priority goal and think about how you can work towards it. If it is a large goal, for instance 'learn Mandarin', try to break it up into concrete and manageable parts. For example, instead of 'learn Mandarin', the goal should be amended to 'experience a Mandarin class and see if it is right for me', with further points:

1. Look up availability and cost of local Mandarin classes.
2. Set aside time to attend Mandarin classes.
3. Book Mandarin classes.
4. Attend Mandarin classes.
5. At the end of one term, evaluate whether I wish to continue to learn Mandarin.

Restructuring actions in this way renders them more achievable and allows us to re-evaluate what it is that we want, rather than setting ourselves up for failure and the possibility of dropping out.

With respect to improving relationships, it is often the case that the relationships that we identify as the most important to us (with our children, our spouse, our parents) are the very ones we neglect the most. Recognising a priority is the first step to change and even if immediate change is not possible, making plans towards this priority is always possible; for instance, although as a speciality trainee I decided to work full-time, ultimately I planned to finish training as soon as possible and to move towards part-time working and my priority goal of spending more quality time with my children. For my corporate husband, who regularly worked until 8–9pm, I came up with a solution for him involving his coming home by 6pm one night a week, and working until 11pm another night to make up the time. In this way, at least once during the working week he could spend quality time with his children. If a relationship is important to you, there are always solutions to be found. Where solutions are not found, more often than not it is because the relationship is not actually a priority, and harder, more searching questions should be asked.

Understanding myself

When I started making my own list of my strengths and weaknesses, the weakness side was long, but I shall share my main one with you as an example to help you on your way in thinking about your own lives. For most of my life, I had an issue with being a Chinese immigrant. It wasn't only kids stretching out their eyes at me and the unkind, racist, immature remarks some people made, but the deep sense of exclusion. As a nine-year-old child, when my best friends bonded over having spent their summer together on a Christian holiday camp, I wished and wished with my eyes tightly closed that I could be white.

When friends came over for playdates, I felt humiliated when they told me that the Taiwanese specialities that my mother prepared 'tasted like toothpaste' and spat them out. Later at university, I felt sick when on the Fresher's Week blind date night, my blind date was the only one who didn't show up. The only thing he knew about me was my 'weird Asian name', and all I could assume was that that was sufficient to put him off. Similarly, my blond friends were invited to join the 'cool' drinking society but I wasn't (neither were my brunette or BME friends), which made more sense when I was told that the selection process had involved looking at the year photo and 'inviting the blonds'. I felt ashamed when housemates told me that 'my food stank' and one time, someone put their used teabag in my leftover katsu curry 'because it looked like sh*t'.

Although initially I attended a few Chinese/Taiwanese society events at university, after a term, I rejected this route and set out henceforth to be as 'British' as I could. This involved wearing cashmere twinsets, silk scarves and listening to ABBA* (dear Lord!), referring to Asian pop music as lame and avoiding eye contact with other Chinese people at parties lest they should approach me, assuming we had something in common.** I'm ashamed to say that at times, it even involved distancing myself from old Chinese friends and my 'embarrassing' parents. This cultural rejection felt necessary for me to fit in, but it wasn't me.

With this background in mind, it is probably easier to understand why an off-hand comment later on in life implying that I was not British had sent me to the brink. The realisation

---

* By my late teens I had moved on to R&B, Indy and Drum and Bass, so ABBA was a bit of a leap, being something my parents listened to. In my adult years I have learnt to love ABBA via *Mamma Mia!*

** This was often reciprocated with great hilarity, as the only two Chinese people in a room would actively avoid each other like the plague.

that others did not view me as British hurt all the more because of all that I had given up in an attempt to be British. For all my received pronunciation and western clothing and culture (I can wax lyrical about the Wombles, Bagpuss, Hockney, the Thatcher years, Wham and Bros), I would never be accepted. What angered me most was that by contrast my white South African husband (who unlike me never supports England in cricket or rugby and runs around screaming 'Bokke' when he gets the opportunity) was immediately accepted as being 'British', when he'd only been in the country a year and didn't even know who Orinoco was or anything about the mouse-organ (apartheid years cultural boycott – I like to think that the Wombles and Bagpuss played their part in bringing down a racist regime). In his mind, the greatest pop act of the 80s was Rodriguez. Who? Exactly (ask a South African). Much as we would like to justify prejudice by citing language, history and culture as objectionable points of difference, more often than not it distils down to skin colour.

Accepting myself

Once I was able to drill down to the root causes of my problems, it was easier to think about what I could and could not change. While I could wish all I liked to be a white male, this was never going to happen. I needed to come to terms with my ethnicity, clear in my head that I shouldn't need to change who I was to fit in with other people. Rather, I needed to find the right people for me, those who liked me for me. There would always be people who saw me only as 'yellow' – some have even suggested that I would taint Andrew's family with my 'yellow babies', but so be it. I realised that in the process of trying to please others, I had shut down whole parts of myself and had staggered on incomplete. I needed to stop seeking validation from others – my parents, my peers, my employers – and instead validate myself: find myself and know that this was enough.

A new perspective

It is important to realise that some of the things that are perceived by society as 'weaknesses', such as having autism, ADHD, dyslexia or a physical disability, or even gender and ethnicity, are also potential positives, and applying a positive reframe is helpful. For me, although being female and Chinese had led to much negative unconscious bias in my career, when I tried to turn my life around, I focused as much as possible on consciously making these attributes an advantage. Rather than trying to anglicise and take on masculine traits (as I had done unsuccessfully in my early career), I focused on authenticity, on being myself.

At conferences I didn't emulate the prominent male colleagues who were adept at 'brown-nosing' senior male academics by asking intelligent but irrelevant questions to show off how clever they were; or try and talk about squash, rugby or golf and make jokes at the expense of others. Instead, I quietly chatted to peers about childcare problems and work–life balance. I bonded with talented women about our universal problems and made real friends and got involved in social networks based on what was authentic to me. In time, these women came to positions of power and they supported their network, including me. Some have given me opportunities and in turn, I have given opportunities to others. What men have been doing for centuries – i.e. elevating opportunities for other men – women can also do for other women. The only snag is that there are fewer women in a position to do so, but I hope that with time and increased awareness, this will change. The same applies for people from other marginalised groups.

Later, working outside the NHS with like-minded people who supported each other opened my eyes to how wonderful a workplace can be. It taught me how colleagues and work environments can be compassionate, flexible and tolerant, and that often it is only by being brave enough to reject what feels wrong that we can find what is right – not just a place where we are tolerated, but a place where we can truly belong.

Once I had made the decision that I was going to put my role as a mother first, I tried not to see it as weakness, or a blight on my career, or hold onto any resentment. I started to write a blog about parenting, in which I shared my real frustrations regarding work-life and domestic imbalances. My blog eventually turned into a parenting book that has since been translated into several languages and led to other opportunities, including this current book. It struck me afterwards that this weakness of 'wanting to be a hands-on parent' was in fact my greatest strength, for without my first-hand experience of parenting, I would undoubtedly be a less sympathetic child psychiatrist, and without the tales of my own parenting struggles, there would have been no books.

Looking back, my blog writing also helped me personally. My ultimate fear lay in the worry that others did not accept me for who I was, and yet, as my blog progressed – and with the support and feedback from my growing readership – I was able to reveal more and more of myself, about my Chinese heritage and how it feels to be Chinese British today. Once a blog is posted, it is read and 'out there' for the scrutiny of others. So just like Ted who had to know that 'Ted Jacobs is a paedophile' was left written on a whiteboard in London, I had to sit at home knowing that my naked feelings were out there in the blogosphere. And just as Ted realised when nothing terrible happened that his worries were unfounded, so I also came to realise that many people were willing to accept me for who I was after all.

Since my negative experiences of unconscious bias, I have tried to stop being a victim about it and instead take the advantages of the positives from my gender and ethnicity. I have become quite adept at shaking my head and saying 'Ah, so sorree – lah. Master no in. I no English,' which I have discovered is a very effective way of getting rid of unwanted door-to-door salesmen and canvassers. If my kids misbehave mildly in public (as children do), I can tut, shake my head and say, 'It's because their parents work such long hours and they don't pay me enough to intervene,' and go back to my coffee and phone (yes, even child psychiatrists do this sometimes – we are human!). I try to avoid confrontation most of the time, but on the rare occasion that it happens, I have found the perfect response to 'Stop using the race card' is 'I'll gladly do so when you stop using your white privilege.'

Another thing that works in my favour is that many institutions are now recognising the need to promote women and BME people, so it's a good time to stress these attributes. The NHS has a Clinical Excellence Award system, and every year, they give many more awards to white males than to any other demographic category, stating shortfalls in applications from BME people and females. Although there are no quotas, they are required to publicly quote the statistics of applications and awards. Therefore, I make a point of applying for this award every single year I am eligible, whether or not I have been 'clinically excellent', just to be counted; and I encourage other women and BME doctors to do this. In doing so, we become visible and counted. Simply by applying, we promote the promotion, if not of ourselves, of other women and BME people. Increase baseline applications, and promotions will necessarily follow.

In this way, by starting to positively reframe my 'weaknesses', I began to accept myself for who I really am, and everything changed. After decades of pretending to be what I thought of as 'British' and shying away from acknowledging important parts of my heritage, keeping quiet about my ethnicity as if it were something to be ashamed of, I was finally out, proud, and shouting about it out loud. I was at last happy in my own yellow skin.

Self-acceptance

Look at your own list of weaknesses and determine which are changeable and unchangeable. For those that you cannot change, for instance a disability or indifferent parents, try and adopt a positive reframe. It is sometimes difficult to imagine, but all weaknesses have a flip-side strength, for example many blind people have enhanced hearing; my patients with ADHD struggle to concentrate, but for some of them, the ability to flit from one topic to another boosts their creativity and lateral thinking; indifferent parents often make you more independent. Taking time to consider the positives and how a bad situation can be improved, exploited or taken advantage of can be helpful. Rather than feeling a requirement to adjust yourself to suit a prescribed view of 'life' and 'success', adjust your vision of what success means to suit you as an individual.

Forgiving ourselves

Cataloguing our life's mistakes and times when we have fallen short is an impossible burden unless we are willing and able to forgive ourselves. I doubt there is anyone who ever reaches adulthood without a single regret. As a child, having recently transferred from a rough school to a middle-class one in the suburbs, I kicked a nice boy in the playground one day 'because I could' and made him cry. I boasted about it to my family that evening, and they were horrified and disapproving. Being shamed for my actions made me apologise to him the next day, but my guilt has stayed with me even today. Accepting our mistakes and forgiving ourselves for who we once were stops us making the same poor choices again and helps us become a better version of ourselves.

Forgiving others

For a while I harboured hatred in my heart over injustices I felt keenly, but I came to realise that this was eating me up and adding to, rather than relieving, my stress. I knew that to move on, I had to let go. This meant understanding the consultant who implied I was not British, the professor who denied me mentorship and the line manager who had bullied me. Over time I have recognised that they, like all of us, were mere products of society, and likely had no particular personal grievance with me.

Gender and ethnicity prejudices and biases are so pervasive that it is impossible for anyone my age or older not to hold one. Consider truthfully if you would have been more or less inclined to buy this book had it been entitled: *A Sense of Belonging*, by Dr Amy Jones. I think that unless you were Chinese, you might have preferred a book by British-sounding Amy. The reason I have some confidence in that statement is because I myself probably would have picked up Amy's book ahead of *A Sense of Belonging*, by Dr Fatimah Akhbar or by Dr Wanjeri Mbugua. Even more likely, Fatimah and Wanjeri would never even have managed to get published (thank goodness for my publishers, who took a chance on Holan Liang).*

---

* While I have seen an explosion of BME female fiction writers, we are

Just to show that racial prejudices and assumptions are rife in all races: when I was a little girl, my mother used to tell me a Chinese bedtime story about the origins of the human race. God was making humans from biscuit dough and a gingerbread man cookie cutter. Unfortunately, the first batch got burnt, the second batch were pale, undercooked with soggy bottoms, but he got it right in his last batch – golden brown and delicious. When I came to the UK, it surprised me that this story was not at all known. You can imagine how it went down at carpet time in my reception class in Wales when the teacher asked about our favourite fairy tales and I put my hand up and said, 'My favourite is the one about God making humans from cookie dough and the golden brown ones were much better than the black and white ones.' Don't worry, I quickly became enlightened to the racism behind this popular Chinese story – I think my four-year-old self mainly liked it because it was about biscuits. But the point is, racism is not only about black and white, and probably all of us, particularly those of us of older generations, hold at least an ounce of it because of the societies we were brought up in. Understanding this, I was able to forgive the people who had discriminated against or hurt me in the past because of my race.

Having spent a lifetime listening to the stories of troubled patients, I really feel that most people never set out intentionally to hurt others – racists and bigots are generally the products of their society; bullies tend to have been hurt, alienated or threatened themselves. If we are looking for solutions, we need to work towards changing systems and society as a whole. What is the purpose of one sacked minister/police chief/CEO/media mogul if they are replaced with carbon copies? The more important question is: are we as a society willing to change?

---

yet to see many non-fiction books by BME women who are portrayed as experts in their fields unrelated to their ethnicity.

Narrative therapy

Writing out our own stories allows us to better make sense of our own experiences, and emotions. On rereading our own personal experiences we are forced to face them and evaluate them more objectively. It can unburden us of pent-up emotions and injustices and allow us to let go, forgive and move on. I certainly found this to be the case in writing this book. Give it a try and see if it grabs you, even if what you write is for your own eyes only. Of course, you might find that you have a story to tell that captivates others and who knows where that could lead?

Finding a voice

Like 'keep a stiff upper lip', 'forgive and forget' is a common piece of inherited advice that we hear, which I feel is a little outdated with regards to our modern understanding of mental health. Although I thoroughly believe in forgiveness and understanding, I really don't see any benefit in 'forgetting'. If we forget, then surely we just continue to repeat the same mistakes and walk in circles, when what we need to do is to learn and move on.

While I have understood the unconscious biases of people who have hurt me and do not hold any personal grudges, it doesn't mean that I should forget or accept the unfair systems in place that perpetuate these biases. Finding my voice has been part of my salvation. I soon found that being proactive is both self-empowering and empowering of others, allowing them to feel more able to add their voices and views too. Doing what you can to challenge the system, however little, gives you a great sense of strength and purpose. Even if our own individual acts are drops in the ocean, together they can cause a tsunami. For me, writing this book and being able to shine a light on mental health stories that are rarely told and highlighting the negative impact of social inequality is my small contribution.

In recent years, I have found myself invited more and more often to a seat 'at the table', at hospital senior management meetings or at the Royal College of Psychiatrists. I now have the confidence to speak my mind, and much to the chagrin of the establishment, I no longer feel embarrassed to ask if gender or race had anything to do with decisions made and I try to highlight system inequalities. Some people may tut or disagree when I voice my opinion, but occasionally there is a buoying 'Hear, hear', and whenever I have felt a fool by breaking the taboo and speaking out, someone or other has always approached me afterwards and thanked me for asking the question or making the point they had in mind but dared not speak. It is these small affirmations of solidarity that keep me going – and if you try this yourself, I am sure they will sustain you too.

Reprioritising my life

These days I divide my working week between the NHS and private practice – the latter allowing me much more flexibility and choice in my hours, so that, for example, I can work only during the school day, and therefore ensure that my children get a good part of me. In addition, I try to remember my own needs: doing yoga, learning to cook Chinese food with my mother and not being afraid to turn down work opportunities that would come at too high a price to my mental health. Life is good for me now. I never gave up on the possibility of a fulfilling career and full-on parenting and, although I was rejected from the system time and time again, I have found my own way and my own place to belong. Recently, several colleagues have told me that they want the working week that I have, combining NHS and private work, writing books, dabbling in research, teaching and policy, and having fun with my kids, while maintaining a comparable salary. It's taken me a lot of sweat, many tears and several teeth, but I now have a career that white males want. How ironic is that?

The answer is blowing in the wind

When I embarked on the journey of writing this book in 2019 with the content already established, I could not have known that in 2021, as I pen the finishing lines, I would find myself part of a tidal swell of human emotions similar to my own, with the need to belong at the heart of it all. The events of the past 18 months have exposed and highlighted injustices and exclusions in different groups across society: the overworked health professionals at the frontline facing burn-out; the victims of systemic racism within the health service; the children whose poorer life opportunities have only been exacerbated during the pandemic; the people who found themselves forced to march in protest against anti-Asian violence in the USA; and the tragic deaths of George Floyd and Sarah Everard. I had worried and wondered for many months if people would want to hear my patients' stories or would understand my own story. I feared I would be taken for an ungrateful immigrant, a bitter, incompetent and 'bloody difficult' woman, but the recent and widespread outpourings of personal experiences of systemic bias and racism, social inequality and the feeling of a wind of change lead me to be hopeful.

To witness communities pulling together to support the frail in society; the unprecedented numbers of those signing up to volunteering services; people of all colours marching across the world in support of social justice and racial equality; women and girls standing up against sexual violence on our streets and in our schools, supported by their husbands, fathers, brothers and friends, has been mind-blowing and heartening. It feels as if despite globally pessimistic circumstances and divisive politics, individual people are demonstrating and calling for change, kindness, compassion and understanding. This makes a difference.

And so, I return to the boy in the cage. On my journey in mental health, I have realised that perhaps at some point in our lives, we will all find ourselves in our own invisible cages, one way or another, entrapped in our own negative life and social experiences and fearful of an unkind world. And as with the boy in the cage, the answer is simple: my mother's brief act of compassion made him smile. It has since made me see that there are only a few mental steps from 'I can't stand you' to 'I understand you' and I think that this is fundamentally what we are all searching for: to be understood, to be accepted, to belong. What if a kinder, fairer, more understanding society could reduce mental health problems? I am sure that it would, and I think that we could get there.

Acknowledgements

Most sincere thanks to one of my oldest friends and long-suffering dentist, the amazing Dr Farah Jessa who made me smile as a child and made my smile as an adult.

This book felt very much like a baby that has taken many years to conceive and deliver. If that were the case, then many thanks to my partner in this endeavour, Laetitia Rutherford, who helped shape the DNA and backbone and held my hand throughout. The team at Watson Little are our extended family, especially proud aunt Rachel Richardson. Thanks also to Helena Sutcliffe, Kristina Blagojevitch and Aurea Carpenter, who like all the best midwives continued to press for me to 'push harder'. Although never appreciated at the time, always appreciated afterwards! Many thanks, the book is much improved because of it. They are of course part of the support from the whole obstetrics team: Short Books, including Rebecca Nicolson, who I am grateful to for taking a chance on promoting diverse stories. Thanks to Katherine Stroud and Becke Parker for their belief and work in promoting the book.

Thanks to my medical school friends who tackled the human and frog dissections and guinea pig ileums on my behalf: Yasmin Reyal, Chat Chierakul, Reggie Li, Tanya Carthy. I continue to attribute my career to the early mentorship of the late Alan Flisher who gave me my first taste of child psychiatry research in South Africa. I am grateful to all the amazing psychiatrists who have taught me over the years, and to the Sun and Doves friends, especially: Jenny Jack, Soraya Mayet, Kimberlie Dean, Michelle Smith, Charlotte Wattebot-O'Brien and Susie Whitwell, and fellow child psychiatry trainees: Gaby Pendlebury, Katya Polyakova, Krishna Menon, Kris Vedi, Daljit Jagdev, Gil Myers, Esra Caglar. Special thanks to an amazing female life-support team: Patricia Rios, Antigone Gkaravella and Isobel Heyman; and the other wonderful women who have offered advice, humour, friendship and support along a turbulent career: Fiona McEwen, Charlotte Tye, Lizzie Shepherd, Eleni Paliokosta, Susie Walker, Jenny Parker and Roz Shafran. Thanks to Farhana Mann for expertise on loneliness and Lisa Mukherjee for advice on eating disorder.

Thanks to Jon Gray for the lovely artwork which visually sums up belonging and finding one's place so neatly.

Most thanks to my friends and family for your lifetime of support: Sue Chuan, Shinn-Chung, Wen-Lan, Chyng-Lan, Jessica, Zoe, Sophie, Fred, Kirsten, Stian, Elsa, Daniel M., Matthew, Almudena, Peggy, Katie, Yuen, Ravi, Emily, Daniel H., Anton.

References

1   Baumeister, R.F., and Leary, M.R. The need to belong: Desire for interpersonal attachments as a fundamental human motivation. *Psychological Bulletin* (1995), 117 (3): 497–529.

2   Liang, H. *Inside-Out Parenting. How to Build Strong Children from a Core of Self-Esteem* (2017), Bluebird Books.

3   Hazan, C., & Shaver, P.R. Attachment as an organizational framework for research on close relationships. *Psychological Inquiry*, (1994), 5 (1): 1–22. https://doi.org/10.1207/s15327965pli0501_1.

4   Maternal depression and child development. Canadian Paediatric Society Position Statement 2004-2003. *Paediatric Child Health* (2004), 9 (8).

5   Rutter M., et al. Quasi-autistic patterns following severe early global privation. English and Romanian Adoptees (ERA) Study Team. *Journal of Child Psychology and Psychiatry* (1999), 40: 537–49.

6   Mental Health of Children and Young People in England, 2017. Government Statistical Service. NHS digital. www.digital.nhs.uk.

7   Dweck, C. Mindset: *How you can fulfil your potential* (2012), Random House Publishing Group.

8   Robinson, S., et al. *Breaking Free from OCD: A CBT Guide for Young People and their Families* (2008), Jessica Kingsley Publishers.

9   Bieling, P.J., Beck, A.T., and Brown, G.K. The Sociotropy-Autonomy Scale: Structure and Implications. *Cognitive Therapy and Research* (2000), 24 (6): 763–80.

10 https://digital.nhs.uk/data-and-information/find-data-andpublications/supplementary-information/2019-supplementaryinformation-files/hospital-admissions-for-eating-disorders; https:// www.theguardian.com/society/2020/dec/29/hospital-admissionsfor-children-with-eating-disorders-rise-by-a-third-in-england.

11 Cacioppo, S., Capitanio, J.P., and Cacioppo, J.T. Toward a Neurology of Loneliness. *Psychological Bulletin* (2014), 140 (6): 1464–1504. doi:10.1037/a0037618.

12 Cacioppo, S., Capitanio, J.P., and Cacioppo, J.T. Toward a

Neurology of Loneliness. *Psychological Bulletin* (2014), 140 (6): 1464–1504. doi:10.1037/a0037618.

13 Wakefield, J.R.H., et al. The Relationship Between Group Identification and Satisfaction with Life in a Cross-Cultural Community Sample. *Journal of Happiness Studies* (2017), 18: 785–807 doi10.1007/s10902-016-9735-z.

14 Loades, M.E., et al. Rapid Systematic Review: The Impact of Social Isolation and Loneliness on the Mental Health of Children and Adolescents in the Context of COVID-19. *Journal of the American Academy of Child & Adolescent Psychiatry* (2020), 59 (11): 1218–39. doi: 10.1016/j.jaac.2020.05.009.

15 Heyman, I., Liang, H., Hedderley, T. Covid-19 related increase in childhood tics and tic-like attacks. *Archives and Disease in Childhood* (2021), 106: 420–1.

16 Mental Health of Children and Young People in England, 2017. Government Statistical Service. NHS digital. www.digital.nhs.uk.

17 Berryman, C., Ferguson, C.J., and Zegy, C. Social Media Use and Mental Health among Young Adults. *Psychiatric Quarterly* (2018), 89: 307–14 doi 10.1007/s11126-017-9535-6.

18 Honeyman, G. *Eleanor Oliphant Is Completely Fine* (2018), Harper Collins.

19 Research Briefing. Oxbridge Elitism. Paul Bolton. (March 2021): https://commonslibrary.parliament.uk/research-briefings/sn00616/

20 Mandai, M., et al. Loneliness among mothers raising children under the age of 3 years and predictors with special reference to the use of SNS: a community-based cross-sectional study. *BMC Women's Health* (2018), 18, Article no: 131 https://doi.org/10.1186/s12905-018-0625-x.

21 Chambers, M., et al. Exploring the emotional support needs and coping strategies of family carers. *Journal of Psychiatric and Mental Health Nursing*, 8 (2): 99–106 https://doi.org/10.1046/j.1365-2850.2001.00360.x.

22 A summary of these classic experiments can be found at: https://www.verywellmind.com/what-is-conformity-2795889.

23 Maenner M.J., et al. Prevalence of Autism Spectrum Disorder Among Children Aged 8 Years — Autism and Developmental Disabilities Monitoring Network, 11 Sites, United States, 2016. *MMWR Surveillance Summaries* (2020), 69 (No. SS-4): 1–12. https://www.cdc.gov/mmwr/volumes/69/ss/ss6904a1.htm.

24 Colvert, E., et al. Heritability of Autism Spectrum Disorder in a UK Population-Based Twin Sample. *JAMA Psychiatry* (2015), 72(5):

415–23. doi: 10.1001/jamapsychiatry.2014.3028.

25 Polanczyk, G., et al. The Worldwide Prevalence of ADHD: A Systematic Review and Metaregression Analysis. *American Journal of Psychiatry* (2007), 164 (6): 942–48.

26 Simonoff, E., et al. Randomized controlled double-blind trial of optimal dose methylphenidate in children and adolescents with severe attention deficit hyperactivity disorder and intellectual disability. *Journal of Child Psychology and Psychiatry* (2013), 54 (5): 527–35.

27 https://www.dailymail.co.uk/health/article-1359679/ NHS-staffrude-arrogant-lazy-Patients-verdict-2-3-tell-poor-care. html; https:// www.dailymail.co.uk/news/article-9123391/National-landmarkscapital-light-blue-celebrate-NHS-frontline-workers.html.

28 Kim-Cohen, J., et al. Prior juvenile diagnoses in adults with mental disorder. *Archives of General Psychiatry* (2003), 60: 709–17.

29 Mental Health of Children and Young People in England, 2017. Government Statistical Service. NHS digital. www.digital.nhs.uk.

30 Morgan, C., Charalambides, M., Hutchinson, G., and Murray, R.M. Migration, Ethnicity, and Psychosis: Toward a Sociodevelopmental Model. *Schizophrenia Bulletin* (2010), 36 (4): 655–64, 2010 doi:10.1093/schbul/sbq051.

31 Morgan, C., et al and the AESOP study group. First episode psychosis and ethnicity: initial findings from the AESOP study. *World Psychiatry* (2006), 5 (1): 40–46.

32 Cooper, K. Minds Apart. *The Doctor* (2020), 25: 18–21.

33 Herzog, D.B., et al. Recovery and relapse in anorexia and bulimia nervosa: a 7.5-year follow-up study. *Journal of the American Academy of Child and Adolescent Psychiatry* (1999), 38 (7): 829–37.

34 https://www.unwomen.org/en/digital-library/publications/2020/04/ policy-brief-the-impact-of-covid-19-on-women.

35 Recommended reading on behavioural activation: https://www.cochrane.org/news/ featured-reviews-behavioural-activation-therapy-depression.

36 Recommended reading on narrative therapy: https://www.apa.org/ ptsd-guideline/treatments/narrative-exposure-therapy.

37 Gray, M., Litz, B.T., and Papa, A. Crisis debriefing: What helps, and what might not. *Current Psychiatry* (2006), 5 (10): 17–29.

38 Gender pay gap references: https://www.gov.uk/government/ Dr Holan Liang 243 news/new-data-on-gender-pay-gap-in-medicine; https:// www.lawsociety.org.uk/about-us; the-law-society-group-gender-pay-gap-report/; https://www.personneltoday.com/hr/

gender-pay-inequality-increases-in-financial-services/.

39 Ethnicity inequality references: https://www.bmj.com/company/
newsroom/pay-of-nhs-doctors-varies-by-ethnic-group/;
https:// www.theguardian.com/media/2017/jul/19/bbc-salary-
datashows-huge-pay-gap-between-white-and-bme-stars; http://
www. pulsetoday.co.uk/news/quarter-of-bme-gps-experience-
patientdiscrimination-at-least-once-a-month/20036640.article;
http:// www.pulsetoday.co.uk/news/all-news/gmc-more-likely-
toinvestigate-complaints-against-bme-doctors/20038897.article;
NHS Workforce Race Equality Standard. 2018 Data Analysis
Report for NHS Trusts; Born Equal? Racism in Medicine. *British
Medical Journal* (2020), 368: 211–60. No 8233 CR ISSN 0959-
8138; Racism in Healthcare: Not just a Covid Problem. *British
Medical Journal* (2021), No 8277 CR ISSN 0959-8138.

40 Moss-Racusin, C.A., et al. Science faculty's subtle gender biases
favor male students. *Proceedings of the National Academy of Sciences
USA* (2012). doi:10.1073/pnas.1211286109; Widner, S., and
Chicoine, S. It's All in the Name: Employment Discrimination
Against Arab Americans. *Sociological Forum* (2011). https://doi.org/
10.1111/j.1573-7861.2011.01285.

41 Wenneras, C., and Wold, A. Nepotism and sexism in peer-review.
Nature (1997), 387: 341–43.

42 Mental Health of Children and Young People in England, 2017.
Government Statistical Service. NHS digital. www.digital.nhs.uk.

43 Slaten, C.D., et al. School Belonging: A review of the History,
current Trends and Future Directions. *The Educational and
Developmental Psychologist* (2016), 33 (1): 1–15. Doi 10.1017/
edp.2016.6; Riley, K. We're a long way from a sense of belonging.
TES Scotland (June 2019), 20–23.

44 *Harvard Business Review*. https://hbr.org/2019/12/
the-value-of-belonging-at-work.

45 Dweck, C. Mindset: *How you can fulfil your potential* (2012),
Random House Publishing Group.

Dr Holan Liang is a consultant child and adolescent psychiatrist at Great Ormond Street Hospital in London, specialising in neurodevelopmental disorders, in particular Tourette's Syndrome, ADHD, Autism Spectrum Disorder and Intellectual Disability. Born in Taiwan, she moved to the UK as a child and studied medicine and experimental psychology at Cambridge, before training in psychiatry and child psychiatry. She has received several NHS Clinical Excellence Awards and her team won the *BMJ* Mental Health Team of the Year Award 2021. As well as lecturing and teaching, Liang has written multiple peer-reviewed research papers and articles for the national press. A mother of two, she published *Inside Out Parenting: How to Build Strong Children from a Core of Self-Esteem* in 2017.